What Really Drives Where We Shop, Eat, and Play

Nora Lee

ULI–the Urban Land Institute
1025 Thomas Jefferson Street, N.W.
Suite 500 West
Washington, D.C. 20007-5201

Lee, Nora.
    The Mom Factor.
    Washington, D.C.: ULI–the Urban Land Institute, 2005.

ISBN: 0-87420-944-7
Library of Congress Control Number: 2004099417

Printed in the United States of America.
10 9 8 7 6 5 4 3 2 1

Dedication

To Jean Wade Turner, for giving me the pen.
To Louise Elliott Lee, for sharing wisdom.
To Matthew and Benjamin Lee, for patience, love, and making me Mom.

About the Author

Nora Lee, catalyst/principal of Nora Lee et al, has been observing and writing on the family entertainment market as a professional and as a Mom for many years. As a content developer, she has contributed her story ideas to clients as diverse as the AOL Time Warner Experience, ObieCo, BRC Imagination Arts, and the Rochester Museum and Science Center. Her articles have appeared in publications all over the world, including *Urban Land* magazine, the *Los Angeles Times, Entertainment Management, American Cinematographer,* and *L'Ecran Fantastique.* She was the editor of *The Basix* for two years and *The EZone* for four years. Lee's lively style and eclectic interests have made her a popular speaker for organizations such as the Urban Land Institute (at its annual urban entertainment conference), the Association of Science and Technology Centers, the American Association of Museums, the Themed Entertainment Association, and the Accademia Internazionale per le Arti e le Scienze dell'Immagine in L'Aquila, Italy. She lives with her family in Altadena, California.

As a note to her audience, Nora Lee writes: If you're a Mom and have a story to tell about a truly wonderful or incredibly awful entertainment experience, or if you would like to comment on something you read in this book, please write to: nora@momfactor.com.

Contents

Acknowledgments

It takes a lot of cooperation, inspiration, and help to write a book. On a project like this, you need an equal amount of cheerleading and butt kicking plus the occasional hot research tip. I would like to thank the following moms, dads, daughters, and sons for their contributions to my success: Michael Beyard, Roger Birkel, Ray Braun, Francesca Chapman, Peter Chernack, Soozi Childers, Susann Edmonds, Pat Esgate, Babette Fuller, Carrie Harris, Emmanuel Lutheran School (William Luedtke, principal), Bennet Kelly, Andrea Learned, Pat McBride, Ernestine Moore, Andrea Randall, Richard Rich, Roy Shafer, Lawrie Stocks, Rick Solberg, The PowerChyx, Helen Thompson, Jody Van Meter, and everyone else who shared a story with me.

In addition, I would like to thank Anita Kramer and the other members of the ULI staff who helped make this book a reality: Rachelle Levitt, Gayle Berens, Nancy Stewart, Lori Hatcher, and Byron Holly; as well as Susan Teachey of ON-Q Design, Inc. The copy editor, Rebecca Bricker, also deserves kudos.

I offer my love and thanks to my son, Benjamin, who makes me laugh and still pats me on the back, and to Judy Wolfram, Jan Harmon, Obie Scott Wade, and Nolan Porterfield for cheerleading above and beyond the dictates of mere friendship.

Most important, I am indebted to my husband Matthew for love, financial support, unwavering belief that this was worth doing, and his vicious red pen. I could not have done this without him.

$\mathcal{P}reface$

What Is a Mom?

What is a Mom? Poets, artists, writers, musicians, and many other creative people have tried to answer this question. A mother is as often fierce and formidable as she is soft and sweet. She comes in all shapes, sizes, and colors. She may have tattoos and piercings or smell of corn silk face powder and wear a girdle. No matter. We all have one—at least one. She has been dissected and diagrammed in psychology books. She has been worshipped as a goddess and reviled as the devil. She can be a source of comfort and warmth or the cause of years of psychiatric bills.

Maybe Mom defies a definitive textbook description, but it's high time she got the attention she's due in one realm, at least—spending money to entertain her family, which, in this book, includes everything from shopping and dining out to theme parks, sporting events, and zoos.

What We Know About Mom

First, we know Moms are women. And we know a lot about women. Statistically speaking, women are not just influential in the marketplace—they control it. It is clear now that even though women still earn less than their male counterparts (about 80 cents on the dollar[1]), they control the lioness's share of the income—not only their own earnings, but, if married, most of their spouses' earnings, too. They choose where to eat, what movies to see, and where to buy jeans and sneakers. According to trend-spotter Faith Popcorn in *Eveolution*, marketing experts Andrea Learned and Lisa Johnson in *Don't Think Pink*, and Martha Barletta in *Marketing to Women*, women are *the* primary decision makers regarding purchases in their households and in their businesses. Between 80 and 88 percent of the buying is done by women.[2] Not only do they make the purchasing decisions on traditional family needs such as clothing and groceries, but also on telephones, Internet services, television and cable, stocks, and insurance policies. That's a lot of feminine financial power.

As women, Moms share in the economic power of their gender. But they should command special attention for two reasons: their sheer numbers and their distinctive purchasing behavior. Of the 108 million adult women in the United States, an estimated 82 million are Moms, and about 32 million of those have children at home.[3] That represents over three-quarters of this feminine financial power, making it essential to understand that Moms think differently, act differently, and certainly spend money differently from our counterparts with no children. The fact that only a certain percentage of the marketplace seems to be aware of the differences between Moms and women is what prompted me to get up on this soapbox in the first place. Examining the research currently available proves my point. There is very little statistical information on the buying habits of Moms—especially in the entertainment areas highlighted in this book.

The lack of specific data means that I am on to a largely unexplored niche. It also means that I have to rely partially on what we know about women to make my case for Moms. Why have Moms received so little formal study? Pat McBride, well-known planning professional and designer of entertainment and destination attractions, points to one reason. Years ago, he says, when his client was the Discovery Zone, "Kids loved it; parents hated it. There was nothing for parents to do while the kids played." He characterized the situation as a disconnect between the user (the child) and the decision-making purchaser (the parent). McBride believes that many developers and retailers pay so much attention to the user that they miss the major influence of the purchaser—Mom. He tells the story of his own family's move to Vermont from Florida. His wife determined that all the kids needed warm jackets, boots, gloves, and scarves for the cold winters. The kids made the style choices, but it was Mom, partly in her role as protector of the family health, who made the overall purchasing decision. To those who gather statistics, it might have appeared that the kids were shopping, but in fact, they were only shopping because Mom insisted, and they were using her dollars. In addition, McBride feels that Mom is no longer happy just seeing a smile on her kid's or husband's face. She wants her own satisfaction out of her retail and entertainment choices. This insight leads to one of the crucial questions I will begin to answer in this book: How do you elicit satisfaction from Mom so that the time and money she spends with you are good for her, and not just one more place to tick off her million-things-to-do-and-places-to-go-to-make-the-family-happy list?

"The movie industry gets it," continues McBride, "It knows Mom is a consumer for herself, so she chooses movies like *My Big Fat Greek Wedding* and *The Hours* and takes her husband along." She also takes her daughter or vice versa. In April 2003, *Los Angeles Times* reporters Michael Cieply and Claudia Eller observed "a new belief that young women are more easily reached by film marketers than are young men." Supposedly, music and video games were drawing off the traditional young male audience, and females were seen as a much more stable group. Further, the authors noted that Dawn Taubin, Warner marketing chief, was targeting the film *What a Girl Wants* to females eight to 16 *and their mothers*. It seems that young girls love to see their favorite movies over and over again, and their mothers often accompany them.[4]

Who is a Mom?

So who is a Mom? The U.S. Census Bureau offers these tidbits:

To begin with, most Moms work. Among mothers 15 to 44 years old who have children over one year old, 72 percent are in the labor force. Even among mothers with infants (under one year old), 55 percent are working.

Not all Moms are married. Ten million are single mothers with children under 18, and that number is rising. (For comparison, there are 2 million single dads, and that number is also rising.)

Most Moms have two children. Only 10 percent end the childbearing years with four or more children.[5]

I'm sure you must have figured out by now that I am a Mom. In fact, I have become an Xtreme Mom, and I'm not ashamed of it either. It's clear to me that my priorities, goals, decisions, and even political activities as a mother are very different from what they were when I was a single woman or a married woman with no children. We 82 million Moms are exerting our power in many ways these days. We vote—remember the Soccer Mom vote that helped reelect Bill Clinton? We own businesses—women are majority owners of over 9 million businesses employing 27.5 million people and generating 3.6 trillion dollars annually.[6] Many women start their own businesses to be able to do something they love and/or to be able to spend more time with their families. It is safe to estimate that more than half of these businesswomen are also Moms. It is Moms in the workplace who insist on flexible work schedules and health care for children.[7] We run for office. In May 2004, there were 59 women serving in the U.S. House of Representatives and 14 in the Senate—both figures at or near historic highs—and 63 percent of these national leaders were mothers.[8] The amazing thing is that these women ran the country while blowing small noses, volunteering at school, and making chocolate milk for their children and grandchildren.

My buying habits changed when I became a Mom, too, and all Moms buy more than just toilet paper and Tylenol. High-tech gear, for instance. CNN.com reports that, according to a survey by the Consumer Electronics Association, women actually spent more on technology in 2003 than men—$55 billion versus $44 billion.

The survey also revealed that electronics stores have been slow to catch on to who their customer really is. (Believe me, they are not alone!) Many still "ignore, patronize, or offend" women shopping for electronic gadgetry. What really frosted 40 percent of the women was that they were treated better when they went shopping with their husbands.[9] So, how do Moms deal with this treatment? Many of the Moms I know go online, do the research, and buy over the Internet. No annoyingly condescending salesman need be present. A 2004 report on online activity surveys revealed that 67 percent of Moms (yes, this was a Mom exclusive!) who were online were researching products to buy. It also showed Moms are squeezing 38 hours of living into their 24-hour days, in part, by using the Internet to do chores or activities.[10] Mom can visit ten stores in 20 minutes online. It might take all day, if she had to drive from place to place.

Surveys and quantitative studies specifically on Moms are rare as hen's teeth, and what there are tell us very little about Moms as purchasing powerhouses. To understand us thoroughly, it's important to understand not just the demographics, but also the way we think. You have to look at individual Moms and listen to the stories we tell. That's why this book is more anecdotal than statistical in its approach. For example, here's a story that every car salesman should listen to:

A vice president of the local community college in our town—a highly respected member of the community and a mother of one—had done her research and was prepared to buy a new Honda. She went to the dealership ready to make a deal. First, she was ignored, and then when she did get a salesman's attention, he opted to talk on the phone to someone about finding a new job, rather than sell her a new car. It was clear to her that because she was a woman shopping alone, she wasn't considered a serious buyer. So she left, and went to the local Acura dealership, which just happened to be owned by a woman. She immediately noted the diversity of the sales staff—women, men, Asians, blacks, and whites—and they genuinely seemed to want her business. A saleswoman helped her pick out a car and, more important, she sold her on attributes that are important to a woman and might not be as important to a man.[11] She explained the safety features of the vehicle and, without condescension, showed her how to use the dashboard buttons. Ka-ching! Remember, this buyer is a mother. Her son is in his early 20s. I predict that when he buys his first car, he won't give that Honda dealership a second glance because of the way it treated his mother. That is just one illustration of the manifold power of Mom. We can point to one lost sale and confidently predict another, but how many other family members will avoid this dealership? How many friends? How many colleagues?

A recent Honda ad campaign featured a busy Mom inundated with family transportation tasks, all characterized by the ubiquitous yellow post-it notes. Her most important to-do note? Go get a Honda Odyssey. And off she goes. But listen, Honda—and anyone else who wants to profit from Mom's business—it is not enough just to talk the talk. If that Mom encounters a patronizing salesperson who fails to accord her the respect she deserves and requires, she's outta there. Selling to Moms (and women in general) can't just be part of the corporate strategy handbook. It has to be implemented on the local, tactical level or it's not worth the paper it's printed on.

You're Going to Be a Mom!

I'll admit that a good part of this book reflects my own experience as a Mom. My transformation into Mom is great cocktail party conversation: My husband and I had been married for over 16 years before we became parents. By then, three different doctors had told me that I wasn't going to have children. So I got a puppy. After all, I was happily married. I truly didn't believe that I needed a child "to complete my feelings of self-worth," as one psychologist suggested. I was a busy professional and a devoted wife.

Then, one January long ago, I started waking up nights to throw up. I couldn't button my jeans anymore, even though I was working out faithfully. After a few months, I took the doctor a list of symptoms that included cravings for salt and milk, mood swings, and swollen feet and ankles. I was sure that I was dying of some strange disease. He suggested that I might be pregnant instead. I assured him that it wasn't even a remote possibility. Three doctors had told me so! He decided to do an ultrasound anyway. Surprise! In August 1990, I gave birth to a lovely little boy. We gave him the name Benjamin (which we had chosen 16 years before—but that's another story).

Having a child fundamentally changed me, my husband, and the way we live our life. Yes, that does that sound like the ultimate cliché! But bear with me.

I never considered myself particularly good mother material, although I think that being responsible for fish, chickens, birds, cats, dogs, and rabbits in my pre-Mom life certainly was good preparation for much of early motherhood. The first years of motherhood are an endless dance of feeding, washing, changing diapers, and walking around in a state of total exhaustion and complete amazement.

Having a child also helped me regain my innocence. It's hard to look at the world cynically when your eight-month-old pats you on the back when you get upset. But for every gain, there was a loss. Things I used to hate, I loved; and things I thought I would love, I hated. The first to go was my sophisticated adult intolerance for noisy environments. If we were going out, then I looked for noisy restaurants, so that if my baby cried, no one could hear him. Next to go was my tolerance for small, badly designed public restrooms. Go ahead—try wrestling a stroller into one of those places. And just where do you leave the baby while you go?

Of course, I also noticed other things. My time seemed to evaporate. I now had a husband, a child, and a career. Juggling became a necessity, not a hobby. I have often thought that there is proof that God is male. If God were female, then we would sprout two extra arms during pregnancy. When our children reached adulthood, they would drop off—the arms, not the children. But that never happens. So our extra arms come from husbands, grandparents, uncles, sisters, cousins, neighbors, nannies—they become the villages that we need to raise our children. And of course, we pay babysitters.

Ah yes, pay. "Pay" by definition means spending money. And parents spend lots of it. How parents—and most important, Moms, because we make 80 percent of the spending decisions—spend money changes enormously over time. In the beginning, it is baby strollers, baby clothes, diapers, baby food, baby locks, baby furniture, and savings bonds for baby. Then it's real groceries for three, movies for three (all G-rated, of course), restaurant dinners for three, baseball gloves for two, music lessons for one, and a new Mom-van to carry one boy, one coach-dad, the gear of an entire T-ball team, two dogs, various grandparents, and snacks. We spend money on Disney videos, computer learning games, tricycles, and health insurance for three. Then we find ourselves buying tickets to the zoo, tickets to Disneyland and Wonderland, tickets to the circus, tickets to Dodgers games, tickets to Texas on an airplane—all times three!

Now we've hit the teenage years and our money is going for new musical instruments, private high school, and scooters with motors and the helmet to protect the precious head. We buy food for four (but there're still only three of us). No more kids menus at our favorite restaurants. No more child discounts, unless we move to England, where childhood ends at 16. New shoes and pants must be purchased every three months because of growth spurts and changing styles. Amp cords, a week at Tahoe with a childhood friend, tickets to Vin Diesel movies, and Dickies pants would never have been on my shopping list, if not for the baby-turned-boy-turned-teen.

It's clear that I am not one of the 10 million single Moms in America. I am blessed with a helpful, loving spouse who has always valued family time. We enjoy our son, and we really get a kick out of going places with him. We seek out "family entertainment," and we have since the beginning. But as my child grew and my career moved in the direction of entertainment real estate, I started noticing that "family entertainment" rarely meant my family. For example, I distinctly remember taking my six-year-old to a newly opened family entertainment center that had been promoting itself as "the place" for families. It was so poorly designed that, once we were through the front door, it was impossible to tell where we were supposed to go. Turned out there was an arcade upstairs, so that's where we headed. I stood in line for tokens, while my husband and son scoped out the games. There were several really violent shoot 'em-ups, a couple of difficult ski and skateboard machines, and the requisite car and motorcycle rides. Nothing age-appropriate for my "family." Ben wanted to ride the motorcycle. I had to help him because he wasn't tall enough to reach all the controls. The only "family game" was a cheesy black-lit miniature golf game, which we played twice.

To add insult to injury, there was no place for Mom or Dad, with pockets full of tokens, to sit and watch their children. It was the first of many times I would find myself thinking, "Wait a minute! You want me to keep doling out money, but you won't even give me a place to sit!" Because there was little for Ben to do, we left within half an hour, with my son shedding tears of frustration.

They didn't want my six-year-old at this family entertainment center, nor did it appear they wanted Moms or dads. So who was their target audience? They never figured it out, and the place closed within months of our visit.

I'm interested in all aspects of marketing to Moms and women in general, but in this book, I want to concentrate on some prominent places where Moms have tremendous influence and yet get too little respect. I won't be talking much about the ins and outs of marketing groceries and cosmetics and similar specific products because marketers in those arenas have at least begun to understand that Moms rule. I will report on whether restaurants, theme parks, museums and attractions, sporting venues, and other places often billed as "family entertainment" live up to their billing. And since malls and a large number of retail stores have added entertainment as a way of enhancing the shopping experience, I'll report on those, too. This is not a book of dry census data, but a book of the real-life experiences of Moms who have spent their hard-earned money and are happy with the experience—or fighting mad because of it. My hope is that in this post-9/11 world, where media attention has made loving your mother and your father and your children seem trendy, what you read here will provide a little insight, or at least prompt questions that have long needed to be asked. The way I see it, wherever business seeks leisure dollars or dis-posable income in this young century, the true secret to its success will be, as it has been for the last century, the Mom Factor.

Nora Lee

Endnotes

1. U.S. Bureau of Labor Statistics, USDL 04-1328, "Usual Weekly Earnings of Wage and Salary Workers: Second Quarter 2004," July 20, 2004, news release.

2. Prerogative Marketing Consultancy, a marketing group in Lawrence, Kansas, evidently did the origi-nal research on this oft-cited statistic in 2002. *Brandweek*, vol. 43, i16, p. 27, April 22, 2002.

3. U.S. Bureau of the Census, American FactFinder Web site (factfinder.census.gov), Quick Tables, Table DP-1: Profile of General Demographic Characteristics: 2000; U.S. Bureau of the Census, American FactFinder Web site (factfinder.census.gov), Detailed Tables, Table P18: Household Size, Household Type, and Presence of Own Children; U.S. Bureau of the Census, Public Information Office, CB04-FF.08, "Facts for Features: Mother's Day: May 9," April 19, 2004 news release.

4. *Los Angeles Times*, Friday, April 4, 2003, pp. C1 and C9.

5. U.S. Bureau of the Census, Public Information Office, CB04-FF.08, "Facts for Features: Mother's Day: May 9," April 19, 2004, news release.

6. U.S. Small Business Administration, "Business Opportunities: Special Interest Topics: Women Entrepreneurs," www.sba.gov/businessop/special/women.html.

7. Richard J. Boden, Jr., "Flexible Working Hours, Family Responsibilities, and Female Self-Employment: Gender Differences in Self-Employment Selection," *The American Journal of Economics and Sociology*, January 1999.

8. www.gendergap.com/government/usc-107.htm. Official government statistics on who in Congress is a mother are unavailable, so I went through the Congressional Directory, 108th Congress (2003–2004, January Online Revision) and counted the women who had children.

9. CNN.com, "Women buy more tech than men," January 16, 2004.

10. The reports were done by Yahoo! Inc., and Starcom MediaVest Group (with data from Just Ask a Woman and TNS Media Research) and by Opinion Research Corp. (for America Online); www.clickz.com/stats/big_picture/demographics/print.php/3351331, May 24, 2004.

11. According to research by J.D. Power and Associates, women show a keener interest than men in safety features, appearance, and recommendations from friends when buying a car. Features that pro-vide driver and passenger comfort are also important to women. Dan Sullivan, Research Associate, J.D. Power and Associates, cited in *Marketing to Women*, vol. 12, no. 10, p. 3, October 1999.

Introduction

What Is the Mom Factor?

Moms are both pragmatic and emotional creatures by design. They feel driven to transform weed-covered lots into playgrounds, both to bring order out of chaos and to give their beloved kids a safe place to play. They help a child realize that bugs have a place in the world, out of appreciation of both practical necessity and nature's remarkable diversity. And Moms make Campbell Soup and Disney mighty brands, both because they feel a comfortable connection with what the names represent and because those companies provide good value. Moms are a force to be reckoned with in virtually any context you would care to name, but it is their economic power in particular that concerns me in this book. In a nutshell, the Mom Factor represents an array of fundamental needs and desires that drive Mom's purchasing decisions for herself and her loved ones. The key to success with Mom is to listen until it *all* sinks in. How many times did your mother tell you to sit up straight or clean your room before you actually did it?

When I began looking for information on how and where Moms spend money, naturally I started with the federal government's Consumer Expenditure Survey. Published by the Bureau of Labor Statistics, it is full of great information about the spending patterns of "consumer units," but I soon discovered its limitations. For instance, the majority of consumer units are labeled "husband and wife,"[1] but there is not a clue about who makes the purchasing decisions. The *gender* of the survey respondents in 2001 is available: 59 percent were men and 41 percent were women. But that doesn't tell me whether it was Mom or Dad who decided to take the family to Hershey Park or the Chicago Bulls game at the United Center. Even the breakdown on entertainment spending is not very helpful for my purposes. The entertainment options I chose for inclusion in this book are spread out among four major categories or are not even mentioned in the survey.

As my search continued beyond the federal data to the private sector, most of the information on Moms got even fuzzier. There is no lack of statistics on women in general—I found studies on women by age, ethnicity, and level of education; on single women; and on women business owners. The Prerogative Marketing Consultancy study that has turned up in everything from doctoral dissertations to the Web site of marketing guru Tom Peters to Faith Popcorn's *Eveolution* indicated that women engage in 80 percent to 88 percent of all consumer spending in the United States. That's incredible! At the lower end, that 80 percent translates into a conservative estimate of $4.6 trillion spent annually by women on goods and services—almost twice the gross national product of Japan.[2] Impressive. Period.

In 2004, the pool of information on women as consumers got a tremendous boost. Two new books spoke directly to marketers on how to take advantage of the tremendous buying power of women: Martha Barletta's *Marketing to Women: How to Understand, Reach, and Increase Your Share of the World's Largest Market Segment* and Lisa Johnson and Andrea Learned's *Don't Think Pink: What Really Makes Women Buy—And How to Increase Your Share of This Crucial Market*. Both books make it very clear exactly who women are, how economically powerful they are, and how to reach them through advertising and marketing. These books are marvelous, insightful guides written by expert marketers for savvy business owners who want to cash in on the single biggest cash cow (it's never a cash *bull*, is it?) in history. When you finish this book, read them. Not only will you gain insight into your customer base, you'll understand your mother, sister, daughter, and grandma much better. However, only *Don't Think Pink* has specific references to Moms as an influential market. And that is as it should be. Demystifying women is the first step in understanding Moms. The authors leave no doubt that women are different from men. But there just isn't much information on how Moms are different from other women. No one has gathered it—certainly not with the kind of focus I was hoping to find.

One of the few major marketing studies I found specifically on Moms was by Jeanie Caggiano and her colleagues at LeoShe, formerly a division of ad agency Leo Burnett.[3] They attempted to analyze the Mom demographic as a way of understanding how to place their clients' products. LeoShe discovered, not surprisingly, that the high priorities for today's Moms include the family eating together, building close relationships with children, expanding kids' horizons, and raising kids with good values. In addition, the agency delineated characteristics for four identifiable segments, each with its distinct psychological profile:

■ **June Cleaver: The Sequel:** This June, JC2, is all Mom all the time and quite happy about it. She doesn't believe that mothers should work outside the home—raising a family is work enough. Dad makes money and she spends it. Eighty-seven percent of the JC2s are Caucasian and they have higher income and education levels than the other Mom market segments.

■ **Tug-of-War:** These are the working Moms who have to be both Mom and bread-winner. They don't like the idea that there's not much time for Mom to be anything else. They are likely to indulge their kids. Forty-two percent are African American and Latina. They represent the lowest income and education levels among Moms.

■ **Strong Shoulders:** These women are resourceful mothers who emphasize learning, growing, and self-esteem with their offspring. There may not be much Dad involvement, but they don't resent that. They like juggling family and career. There are no significant ethnic skews here, and their income and education levels fall between those of June Cleaver and Tug-of-War.

■ **Mothers of Invention:** These are the idealists who believe it is possible to have a happy family and a happy career. They see Dad as an equal partner in parenting. They are somewhat upscale, but span income and education groups. Up to 78 percent are Caucasian.

Whether or not the LeoShe analysts nailed the segments doesn't really matter to me as much as the inferences we can draw from their research about Moms as a group. The most obvious is that all these mothers spend money on behalf of their families—some to excess. All these mothers have tough, busy schedules with a wide variety of duties and demands. All these mothers are striving to do the best they can with what they have. These attributes cross ethnic, education, and socioeconomic lines. To me, it is important to understand the characteristics of all Moms as a major segment of women before we start trying to understand June Cleaver or the other subsets. But I'm very glad that this research has begun.

Besides the LeoShe study (the large exception that proves the rule), the limited coverage of Barletta, Johnson, and Learned, and a scattering of other studies here and there, I found very little solid information on Mom per se that applies to the topic of this book. (It might be worth noting that since my formal research began in 2000, there actually has been an uptick in the number of studies, books, and articles looking at Mom as buyer—just not in my chosen areas.) Of course, sometimes the most significant thing you can discover is nothing. No information can be as telling as limitless information. Everywhere I turned, I had to admit that the Mom stats I wanted just weren't there. Yet something real is out there—something important. My antennae are up and quivering: Moms are so far from recognition as purchasing powerhouses that most people paid to ferret out trends and patterns in economic data apparently don't even know they're there! Or if they do know they're there, they haven't been able to convince their clients to act on the information.

Why Are Moms So Special?

No one with any life experience would argue against the fact that Moms' spending patterns are quite different from those of women with no children. Our own personal experiences as mothers, daughters, husbands, and fathers tell us that. Moms, unlike any other group of women, buy not only for ourselves, our husbands, and our parents, we also buy for our children and eventually our grandchildren. Like women across the categories, we spend the money we make (and 30 percent of working wives make more than their husbands, according to a recent study[4]), and those of us who are married also spend the money our husbands make. And, like women everywhere, we spend not only on the traditional groceries, drugs, and clothes (sold by retailers who at least try to understand us), but also on health insurance and health equipment, airfare and appliances, computers and cars, and entertainment. What sets us apart is that we make all these buying decisions for an average of three additional people!

Let me lay this out clearly: Roughly three-quarters of the adult women in the United States are Moms, according to the 2000 U.S. Census. If we accept that oft-repeated estimate that women account for at least 80 percent of the buying decisions in homes, then it is reasonable to assume that on any given day, well over half the consumer buying decisions made in this country are made by Moms. That market is larger than any single ethnic group or age group or income group or education group. Moms have tremendous financial power! So why do so few companies acknowledge us?

In this book, I argue that if you're a retailer, developer, restaurateur, theme park or attraction operator, museum director, or sports team owner, you should be paying attention to Mom for two main reasons:

■ We decide directly where to spend billions of dollars annually for the whole family's entertainment, not just ours.

■ Our circle of influence is large—we deeply affect brand loyalty in our children and spouses and countless others. We *are* the word-of-mouth every marketer dreams of.

It is important to realize that we aren't talking about the original June Cleaver. I doubt there are five women in the whole United States who do dishes in a full skirt, petticoats, and high heels. We've come a long way since June's day. As Caggiano says, Moms "are smarter, sharper, and far more cynical. This is a generation with a bullshit meter that will go off at the slightest provocation."[5] Needless to say, I'm provoked! Today's Moms are complex and not easily categorized, but I contend, nevertheless, that the vast majority hold certain identifiable values in common: the elements of the Mom Factor.

Listen to Your Mother

Say you're a businessperson who decides to heed my words and pay attention to Mom; how do you go about it? Well, the first step is to find out what Mom needs and wants, right? If you are an entrepreneurial Mom, don't be afraid of your instincts. Implement those ideas that appeal to you as a Mom. If you aren't a Mom, start with an informal survey of those in your circle to see if they have any "off the top of my head" suggestions. In addition, continue reading. There are some answers here.

Notice I did not say *all* the answers. This is not the *Gospel According to Mom* or the *Encyclopaedia Maternica*. It is one Mom/businesswoman's analysis of a very complex subject, based on over a decade of professional scrutiny and careful thought. As you have already seen, it draws on quantitative public sources such as the U.S. Census and the Bureau of Labor Statistics and on market research and previous studies. But because hard data on Moms, per se, are so scarce, the most important information source for this book has been the Moms themselves. Over the past ten years, hundreds of Moms have shared with me their likes and dislikes in shopping, entertainment, and education experiences. In 2002, I took a more systematic approach and sent a detailed questionnaire to some 200 primarily suburban middle-class and upper-middle-class Moms—the kind of consumers that stores and restaurants and museums and theme parks ought to drool over. Returns from this small pilot survey were light (about 20 percent), but analysis of the responses confirmed many of the conclusions I had reached based on other sources, and added a few fine points. I do not claim that my findings are based on statistically random samples. You will find no probit analyses or even t-tests here. But I believe that the patterns I have identified are strong and consistent enough to warrant close attention. Listen to your Mom!

The Mom Factor Checklist

The Mom Factor represents my distillation of what Mom needs and wants. It is composed of 11 separate but related elements. The application of each element varies depending on the venue and buying decision involved and on the life stage and period of history in which Mom finds herself. But none should be ignored because the bottom line is simple: If you build it so that *Mom* will come, she will bring everybody with her and they will love it, too. If it's good for Mom, it's good for others.

1. Health and Safety: Planting the Seeds of a Customer Dynasty

Mom cares about the health and safety of her kids above all, so this would seem to be a no-brainer. But Moms can see danger around every corner. Spills in the aisle, cholesterol-laden food, inedible decorative plants, rickety roller-coaster wheels, bad sightlines at the arcade, nasty restrooms at the stadium all represent a very slippery slope. Mom thinks, "I'm going to give you one chance and if you blow it, not only will I not come back—you can be sure I will tell my friends." On the other hand, if a business provides quick cleanups, appetizing healthy food alternatives, barriers to overinquisitive fingers, evidence of regular safety inspections and maintenance, a clear view of the little ones, and sparkling restrooms, it might well have a customer for life or, even more important, the beginnings of a customer dynasty with Mom at the center. Mom's concern for health and safety is constant, no matter where she takes her kids.

2. Customer Service: The Pot of Gold at the End of the Rainbow

Mom says, "Pay attention to *me*," but often in a soft, self-deprecating voice. *Listen!* She knows perfectly well that she has choices in where to have the kid's birthday party or where to grab a bite before band practice, and the service a business shows her and the kids can make all the difference. Snooty waiters who prefer adults lose both tips and repeat business, but the waiter who brings the toddler some crackers and the first-grader a set of crayons—without being asked—is golden. In good mall design, service and safety include a well-marked pickup and dropoff location for the teens who don't want to be seen with Mom. The clerk who is empowered to make a decision on a return or a sale price beats the heck out of "Duh, I'll have to get the manager, who might be back after lunch." Customer service is a constant concern for Mom because good customer service saves her *time*—the most precious thing on the planet. It also makes the time she spends much more pleasant. These two attributes are worth money to her. She might sometimes be willing to trade off a little service for excellent value (see below), but a business had better make sure the case for the tradeoff is compelling before it risks losing her for good.

3. Value: Cheap Does Not Always Equal a Good Deal

No surprise here. Moms, like most human beings, have only so much money to spend. However, their job description requires them to get the most bang for their buck. They enjoy shopping for a good value at a good price. In fact, from Beverly

Hills, California, to Greenwich, Connecticut, value shopping has become more trendy. Some of the wealthiest among us can be found at Target on a Saturday afternoon. Mom's idea of value translates to a balance of reasonable prices, decent quality, and good selection. Just as a Mom will pay more for good customer service, so will she pay more for good quality, but it's always a balancing act. Cheap flip-flops make sense for one summer of beach-going. But it might be worth it to get a good, warm, more expensive coat (maybe a size too large) to last her youngest the whole winter. Mom's value monitor, like the ones for health and safety and customer service, is a constant across all spending, not just retail. A small watery soda that costs four bucks at the ball game, a $40 investment in tickets to a scratchy print of a large-format film at the museum, $50 times four just for tickets for a family visit to a theme park overrun by poorly controlled crowds or directed by unpleasant ride operators—all these experiences can ruin the day, and make it unlikely that Mom-the-ATM will ever return. Yes, once Mom and the family are in the gate at most venues, she is a captive audience. But if you want repeat business from her, the key to success is DON'T make her feel that way. That, too, is value.

4. Efficiency: When Money Buys Time

Mom's time is precious to her and to her family. Business ought to respect it, by making shopping and spending as efficient and painless as possible. That means everything from the parking lot to the cashier, from the online flight bookings to the signage within the hotel, from the exhibit information kiosk to stroller availability. Last I checked, wasting time is not high on anyone's list, and that goes double for Mom—because she has exactly 22 minutes to get that T-shirt and skateboard grinding wheels before she has to fly to Baja Fresh for a snack for the kids, who have soccer practice on the other side of town in 49—no, 48 minutes. If she can take care of three things at one place instead of one thing at each of three places, that's probably what she'll do—just to save time. Efficiency does not replace customer service; it's more like a service extension. That's why grocery stores now have banks and Jamba Juice; and banks have a Starbucks; and ATMs sell stamps—for those moments when time is of the essence. It's often a little thing. For instance, there are grocery chains in the United States and the United Kingdom that actually listened when Moms asked them to remove the gum and candy impulse items from the checkout areas. Moms were tired of ending their trips to the store in a battle with the kids over the "I wannas!" Grocery shopping instantly became more pleasant and more efficient.

5. Social and Community Conscience: Why Pink Ribbons Work

Moms have always been the most effective and vociferous consciences of their communities—just take a look at *Lysistrata*, for example.[6] But I believe Mom today is more likely than she used to be to base day-to-day buying decisions, in part, on her perception of the social and community responsibility of the businesses she patronizes. Attractions that don't glorify violence will get the nod over those that do. Those that promote a sense of community are preferable to those that isolate the kids or set them against each other. Giant discounters that hire the differently abled or give a set portion of their profits to local schools are more likely to see Mom repeatedly than those that do not. Products displaying pink ribbons attract attention and dollars because Mom's mother or aunt or sister had breast cancer. She'll drive the extra miles to take the kids to the family entertainment center that is holding a fundraiser for the Humane Society because then her role as cheerleader and as a purse with legs has some meaning. And if she is so inclined, she has an opportunity to give one of those Mom speeches about putting your money where your mouth is. Those businesses that demonstrate a social and community conscience have a leg up on those that don't.

6. Story: The Stuff That Dreams Are Made Of

The value to Mom of telling a good story applies especially, but not only, to entertainment and education venues. Theme parks represent perhaps the most obvious example of the role of storytelling in persuading Mom and her family to part with some dollars. Each theme in a theme park *is* a story—the wonder of the oceans at SeaWorld, or the Lost Continent at Universal's Islands of Adventure, for example. The best stories share certain characteristics: they are personal, authentic, engaging, immersive, and memorable. At a zoo, establishing a personal connection with an orangutan named Clyde, who's 22 years old, loves blueberries, and has a jealous mate named Audrey, helps both Mom and child immerse themselves personally in Clyde's story and, more broadly, in the story of a Southeast Asian forest habitat in danger. Seeing Clyde up close in his natural habitat lends an air of authenticity to the experience, and engaging human emotions in the service of learning can turn a visit to the zoo into a lifelong memory. On the other hand, impersonal presentation, fakery or excessive artificiality, physical or emotional distance, and sheer tedium all contribute to a regrettable experience. Quite honestly, those kinds of experiences often create lifelong memories, too—but for all the wrong reasons.

Story helps not only in theme parks, zoos, museums, and attractions, but to a lesser extent in malls, stores, restaurants, and sporting events. Think of the Forum

Shops in Las Vegas, which transports you to Italy, or the Gaslight District in San Diego, which nicely reflects the history of the community within which it is situated, or Yankee Stadium and the legend of Babe Ruth. I'd even say that the flashing lights and the thunder that accompany the misting of produce in many grocery stores represent a kind of storytelling. A good story can transform almost any ordinary occasion into an unforgettable one.

7. Comfort: Now, It's Personal

OK, my feet are killing me, and I've spent $213 for bags full of stuff that are now dragging me down. Where do I sit down for a minute? How about my kids, who of course have all the energy I lack? Mom wants to be comfortable, and she wants her kids and their grandma and everybody else in the group to be comfortable, wherever they go. If the teens are going to ride the death-defying, scarier-than-three-weeks-worth-of-laundry roller coaster, then Mom better have a place to sit where she can see them, or meet them when they come out. If the tweens are going to play video games in the family entertainment center while Mom supplies the tokens, then Mom does not need to be leaning on the wall like a dispenser or hanging over them like a spectre. She needs a place to buy a latte and watch the action. Is it a creative abomination to put benches in an art museum so that one can sit and contemplate the meaning of it all? Mom wants clean restrooms and plenty of them, good ventilation and smoking control, effective queue management, tables that don't smash Dad's knees when he sits down, room to maneuver around racks of merchandise, and maybe even a peaceful place to retreat to for a few minutes, before tackling the to-do list again. Comfort is sometimes a luxury Mom has no right to expect, as in the after-Christmas sale at Loehmann's. But before you cut benches from the budget, consider that a tired, grumpy, footsore Mom is bent on only one thing— getting out of there! Invest in her comfort and she will invest in you.

8. Learning and Teaching Opportunities: The School of Mom

Mom teaches her kids every day of her life. It's a fundamental part of being a Mom. She can't do it alone, of course, and gets assists from Dad, the school, Grandma, other kids, and even PBS. Indeed, she'll take all the quality help she can get and will go out of her way to take advantage of teaching and learning opportunities wherever they arise. Mom loves a good museum, zoo, or aquarium, of course. They're supposed to provide enlightening educational experiences presented in an entertaining fashion. And state and national parks with fine signage and visitor centers are a hit with her. But she looks for education elsewhere, too: the milking display at the county fair, the furniture factory tour, the traveling display on the life of

Ray Charles at the mall, the hayride outside of town, Great Moments with Mr. Lincoln at Disneyland, and Hall of Fame displays at the football stadium. Why, naming fruits and vegetables with the kids at the farmer's market is an educational experience! Even restaurants can offer lesson opportunities, if Grandpa draws on the paper tablecloth while the little ones watch, or the décor consists of World War II flyers' memorabilia. Engaging educational experiences at explicitly educational institutions are a must, but educational value is a wonderful bonus in other venues.

9. Fun: The Pursuit of Amusement Equality

Mom likes to have a good time. No, really, she does! She isn't sister to the Wicked Witch of the West. Dad and Granny and the toddlers and tweens all like to have a good time. For Mom, who takes the responsibility to plan nearly every family outing, the ideal destination is one in which every single family member has some fun—or at least does not suffer from the dreaded B-word: Boredom. Whether that destination is a family entertainment center, museum, local mall, sporting event, or the beach, Mom aims for the most fun for the most people, and all too often sacrifices her own enjoyment for that of others. After all, she knows firsthand the cost of disappointment; it's written on the faces of those kids. The destination that helps her in her quest will win her dollars and her loyalty. The one that considers her own pleasure and then delivers will win her devotion—and a small shrine on which she will place generous offerings of chocolate and comfortable shoes!

10. Continuity and Change: Baby, Don't Ever Change . . . Much

People are funny. On the one hand, they crave novelty. Babies' attention is drawn to changes in their field of vision. Toddlers seize whatever rolls by them and stuff it in their mouths. Preschoolers gaze at the world with rapt attention, trying to assimilate all that's strange and wondrous into their limited framework of experience. Schoolchildren and teens leap on the next cool thing with a vengeance. Adults, too, are attracted to the new model, the new-and-improved soap, the new movie down at the Rialto. Variety really is the proverbial spice of life. Yet at the same time, people love traditions—especially family traditions—with the same degree of delight. Kids, in particular, often insist on certain holiday menu items, birthday rituals, favorite family restaurants, and annual vacation destinations because they're comforting, familiar, and full of memories.

This paradoxical appeal of both change and continuity has a special fuzzy place in the Mom Factor. Mom likes variety and a degree of cool, to keep the kids interested. So the new ride at Disneyland is a good thing. So are an array of choices on the café menu, and spring fashions, and the new joey at the zoo. But you're in peril if you mess with the Tiki Room and its animatronic birds, or white Jockey Classics in the boys department, or the meerkat habitat that has always been at the entrance to the zoo. The new stuffed koala is fun, but you've never seen passion till you witness a five-year-old faced with the disappearance of old Teddy. Businesses cannot remain static, of course, any more than people can. Moderation in all things, said Poor Richard. A balance between change and continuity is necessary to keep Mom and her family happy. If change is for the better, then make sure better is really better.

11. Connection to the Heart: A Moving Experience Doesn't Mean Installing an Escalator

Notice the skein of words that runs through most of the first ten elements of the Mom Factor: Care, concern, conscience, community, wonder, engagement, love, comfort, fun, enjoyment, loyalty, pleasure, delight, and passion. These words all denote a personal, emotional connection between Mom and her world. In an increasingly impersonal, technology-addicted society, Mom is the touchstone for matters of heart. Even in commercial transactions, Mom takes things personally. If a business demonstrates disregard for the safety of her kids, or inattention to its own responsibility to her community, or disrespect for her or her family, she won't just turn away—she'll get *angry*. Hell hath no fury like a *Mother* scorned.

So there you have it: the Mom Factor in checklist form. Hey, I'm a mother. I just know these things.

Endnotes

1. U.S. Department of Labor, Bureau of Labor Statistics, Report 966, "Consumer Expenditures in 2001," April 2003, Table 5; www.bls.gov/cex/csxann01.pdf.

2. Phyllis A. Katz and Margaret Katz, "Purchasing Power: Spending for Change," *Iris: A Journal about Women*, April 30, 2000, no. 40.

3. www.leoshe.com.

4. *Newsweek*, May 12, 2003, p. 46.

5. Lisa Moskowitz, "What Kind of Mother Are You?" Salon.com, February 28, 2000.

6. In this Greek comedy, written by Aristophanes in 411 B.C. while Athens and Sparta were at war with each other, the women of Greece, led by the Athenian Lysistrata, agreed to go on a sex-strike to force their husbands to make peace. They succeeded.

Chapter 1

"Mom, I Gotta Have It!"

hopping for shoes for a growing almost-teenage boy is always an adventure. We have to consider style, color, price, and whether or not we should get two pairs a size apart. I just can't spend a lot of money on the silly things because, no matter what, I'll be back in three months for another pair. So I try to shop sales. There's a major sporting goods store that is always having a shoe sale. The shoe departments tend to be very unorganized and way understaffed by the kind of people who can help you pick out a tennis racket, but don't know diddly about footwear. But I'll sacrifice a lot of service for a good price on good shoes. On one particular occasion, my son had spotted a shoe—yes, just one—on the shelf. It was his size and the right color and "just what I gotta have, Mom." Great. I asked the only person I could catch where I could look for the other shoe. Notice: I was willing to do the looking, I just wanted to know where I should look. His answer was a classic, "I don't know." And he dashed off. So I tracked down the manager. He had no idea either and defended the sales clerk. So I left. I don't buy shoes there anymore. Why should I pay for insults and confusion when I can get them for free so many places?

This chapter is different from those that follow because retail is different. For instance, it's only in the last 20 years or so that retail has entered the realm of entertainment. In the past, we had specialized stores that matched various needs. Most of us bought clothes, shoes, sheets, towels, and bread when we needed them, not for fun or recreation—unless we were very rich. No longer is that always true. Shopping is what two-thirds of us choose to do on our vacations! Many malls have reinvented themselves as destination attractions. Mall of America, one of the best-known shopping centers in the world, offers shoppers airline and hotel packages that include discounts and attractions within the mall. Cherry Creek Shopping Center in Denver, Colorado, also has tourism packages. Many of the malls owned and operated by Taubman Centers, Inc., offer tourists shopping and cultural packages. Orlando and Las Vegas know to include shopping as an attraction when courting tourists.

On the local scene, our teens certainly understand shopping as recreation. Malls, since their inception, have been teen hangouts. We are teaching kids at a very young age that when they're looking for fun, they can go to the mall. After all, it has food, movies, music, and clothes. Often nowadays, it also has rock climbing and ice skating or rollerblading, among other attractions (see Chapter 2). It might even have live performances or contests. It's not just about buying a pair of underwear anymore. Often, shopping is now a choice we make when deciding how to spend leisure time and leisure dollars.

But does it work? Does turning shopping into entertainment influence Mom, who makes so many of the shopping decisions? Will she buy Nikes at Niketown because it's such a cool place, or will she buy Nikes at Famous Footwear because they are so highly discounted? Will she go out of her way to the Billabong store because her teenager loves the atmosphere, or buy that Hawaiian shirt at Target? Does entertainment value—or giant selection or exotic locale—outweigh poor customer service? On what factors do Mom's decisions depend in the retail world?

We've got a lot to talk about.

To distinguish yourself as a retailer in order to attract these mothers and get them to become loyal customers, the all-important first step is to understand why and how Moms shop. The next is to understand the circumference of Mom's circle of influence in the marketplace. And finally, it is important really to understand what customer service means to Mom.

The Shopping Continuum

For Moms, shopping is a continuum. On one end is the kind of necessary shopping that goes on the To-Do list: Target, Wal-Mart, Costco. On the other end of the continuum is shopping just for fun, say at the Venetian in Las Vegas or at Downtown Disney. One step up from Target might be traditional mall shopping. One would still find this kind of shopping on the To-Do list, but a mall would offer a few more amenities and greater selection, if not convenience or value. Nearer the other end of the continuum—the fun end—is shopping at a lifestyle center like Los Angeles's The Grove. It's not the first stop when Mom needs to buy shoes for the kids, but she can go there on a weekend for dinner and a movie and some leisurely shopping. And, of course, there are a dozen different experiences in between.

To-Do Shopping

My research indicates that for most mothers, especially ones with young children, most shopping is neither pleasant nor particularly unpleasant. It simply has to be done. Let's look at this drudge stuff first because it's something we all deal with, it's regular and time-consuming, and it has its own set of challenges for Mom.

So what does a mother look for when she is To-Do shopping, and where does she go? From my own survey and those of other researchers, it is clear that most Moms are looking for anything that makes their lives easier, no matter what they're shopping for. That means they want good customer service and good value—quality, price, and selection. In other words, they are no different from any other shopper. These characteristics form the Holy Grail of any shopping experience along the whole continuum. Ideally, we'd like it all. But on the To-Do end, we are often willing to sacrifice customer service for better value. This partly explains why the women in my survey chose Target, Wal-Mart, and Kmart as their favorite family retail stores.

These stores offer a huge selection of types of items. For Moms, huge selection means loading the kids into and out of the car one time, not three. It means I can buy toothpaste, juice boxes, razor blades, T-shirts, Nerf guns, dog food, garbage bags, light bulbs, lipstick, and a new Dixie Chicks CD in one stop. Anything that saves precious time without too much pain will get a thumbs-up. As Faith Popcorn says, "Time is the new money: people would rather spend money than time." The only major complaint about these value and convenience heavens from the Moms I surveyed—and it was almost universal—was that the customer service is lousy. More on that shortly.

Besides customer service, ideas for improvement that come up often in moth-
erly descriptions of shopping experiences are maneuverability (Moms are often
pushing something with wheels), stocking shelves well, honoring sale ads, and making returns easy. None of this is news to retailers. At least, none of it should be. But
those who know about the problems don't appear to be doing enough about them,
if Moms are still citing them as impediments to shopping enjoyment. Think about
the possibilities for the retailer who can remove those impediments.

Enter Kohl's. Kohl's Department Store is a Menomonee Falls, Wisconsin–based
company that is starting to worry Target, Wal-Mart, JCPenney, and Sears. Part of its
stores' appeal is that they know and actively seek out a Mom-centered demographic. The company builds outside traditional malls in urban areas thick with Moms
between the ages of 22 and 45. It offers great prices and convenience—just like the
above-mentioned companies. However, each store is arranged in a racetrack style
that is supposed to make access and maneuverability a cinch. It eschews big, bright-
ly colored shopping "wagons" —which don't fit two on an aisle or maneuver around
clothing racks—for sleek black carts, strollers, and wheelchairs that make shopping
a more pleasant experience. Exchanges can be made with or without a receipt.
Imagine that! Kohl's sells clothes for the whole family, home furnishings, and small
appliances in brands that are a cut above those carried at Wal-Mart and Kmart.
Analysts say the combination of 80 percent brand names, low prices, and customer
access make Kohl's an investor's darling. It had 597 stores in mid-2004, and its sales
exceeded expectations. The store's tagline is "Shop Happy. Leave Happy," and it
seems to be working for most customers. Retailers that emphasize the To-Do list
can't be expected to make every Mom feel thrilled to go shopping for socks and
a toaster. But the Kohl's concept demonstrates that shopping for necessities can be
nicer than we've come to expect. At least it is a relief to find a retail company that
recognizes that there is a way to make money and offer all the things its primary
customer wants.

However, let me offer a cautionary note: The corporate concept is only as good
as its execution by local management. The Kohl's I visited most recently was very
disorganized, shelves were in disarray, help was impossible to find, and prices
were missing on many items. It was doubly disappointing because of all the hype
surrounding Kohl's. My experience only proves the rule that the corporate
initiative might come from exactly the right place, but implementation and over-
sight are crucial.

The Other Kind of Shopping

There's a second kind of shopping that is fun. You can identify this type simply by asking a few questions, such as: "Is this shopping trip on my To-Do list?" If the answer is no, then chances are you're shopping for fun. "Do I have a schedule to meet?" If the answer is no, not really, then that also indicates shopping for fun. "Where have I chosen to shop?" If the answer is Wal-Mart, then this trip probably isn't for fun. If the answer is Reston Town Center in Virginia, or The Grove in California, then it probably is for fun (see Chapter 2 for more information on lifestyle centers). "Am I happy and relaxed or rushed and tired?" Well, you get the idea.

When a survey reveals that 63 percent of people on vacation shop, the first question that comes to my mind is, "Why?"[1] It's clear that Americans spend an awful lot of each week shopping. Why would they choose to do so on their vacation? For me, the distinction is clear. If I'm on vacation and I choose to shop, the pleasure comes from the pace, the selection, and the unique shops (or at least ones that are different from those I normally go to). Most important, shopping on vacation becomes a way of making and sharing memories, so I'm much less concerned about value—or at least the typical monetary definition of value. The value I'm searching for on vacation is less tangible.

Think of your first trip to Disneyland. Doesn't everyone who goes to Disneyland buy a hat? I would bet that most often they buy Mickey Mouse ears of some variety. Who in their right mind would wear those ears after they have left the park? But most of us keep those ears buried in a closet somewhere, and whenever we run across them, the ears dredge up all sorts of wonderful memories, and we smile. That is their value. The ears become a touchstone to a memorable and authentic event we shared with people we love, and we'll keep those ears forever. Have you ever seen Mickey Mouse ears in a yard sale?

We also like to share special moments with those who can't be there with us, so we buy presents when we're on vacation. If Granddad couldn't come with us, then we send him a silly T-shirt or a shot glass or a rubber lizard with pink sunglasses to let him know we were thinking of him. We also special-occasion shop in this relaxed atmosphere, buying early Christmas or birthday presents. And this is one time when Moms feel reasonably comfortable rewarding themselves. Yes, they will make sure everyone in the family gets something to remember the trip by, but they'll also spring for a new hat or new earrings or a pretty box for themselves, though they might need a little push. The retailer who helps persuade Mom that it's okay to indulge herself reaps rewards for the accomplishment.

The good feelings associated with shopping on vacation, which comes but once a year for most folks, help explain the throngs of people who flock to The Grove in Los Angeles on a weekly basis. Places like The Grove, most of them built since the late 1990s, manage to tap into that feeling of vacation freedom by making shopping part of the entertainment. The new breed of lifestyle centers, with their emphasis on architecture, food, and entertainment, do make a difference in the shopping experience.

In a well-designed environment such as The Grove, it is tricky trying to consider the individual retailer separate from its location. In Chapter 2 on malls, you'll see how important the retail mix is to the success of the place. It is important to understand that the *place* is just as important to the retailer. Both the developer and the retailer know this going in. Developers in recent years have tried to do their homework and define the demographics of the area in which they build. In addition, they have tried to attract tenants that will appeal to the widest possible cross section of that demographic. Sometimes it works and sometimes it doesn't, as you'll see in Chapter 2.

Certain national and regional retailers do make shopping feel more like entertainment or an event. Some that come to mind are Anthropologie, Restoration Hardware, Barnes & Noble, Upstart Crow, Billabong, and Illuminations. In each case, the sales staff is fairly well trained and mostly courteous, the products somehow strike an emotional chord, and children aren't shunned.

Now I know that not all these businesses have fared well with investors. Restoration Hardware, for example, is closing stores. Some analysts believe they built too many stores too soon and in places that couldn't support their particular inventory. I don't know what might save Restoration—fortunately I'm not writing an investment guide—but I would argue that its appeal for Moms kept those stores going longer than they otherwise would have. Retailers will win in the long run if they create shopping experiences that Moms, in particular, enjoy so much that they look forward to going back.

The Billabong Store (the first in the United States) in The CAMP in Costa Mesa, California, is a real eye-opener. There is an enclosed halfpipe for skateboarders, a wave pool for testing surfboards and other equipment, videogames on computers, and, amazingly enough, decent prices on good-quality clothes. Obviously, I went to the store with my teen, but the staff treated me like the Queen Mother I am, and I responded by buying a lot of clothes for my son, a birthday present for a teen friend, and another for Dad—and believe me, neither gift was on the To-Do list.

My son got a kick out of the halfpipe and really wished he had brought his mountain board. He loved the idea of the wave pool, and, of course, he had to sit down in front of the computer for about ten minutes, just to check it out. I loved the way my husband and I were treated. Our questions were answered. We were shown merchandise we might be interested in. We were happy. They were happy. We lingered and actually shopped. We spent money. In fact, we were there for close to an hour, which is unheard of in most retail establishments.

Lingering and spending money have long been linked in the minds of retailers and developers. Studies, first done by Disney, have shown that per-capita sales are directly related to length of stay. That's one of the main reasons that a store goes out of its way to create an atmosphere. If it can keep your attention longer, you are much more likely to spend money. Billabong certainly gets it.

Anthropologie does, too. The stores of this subdivision of Urban Outfitters are, as my mother-in-law would have said, pleasing. The colors and layout and mix of items draw me in like a fish on a line. Each one of the more than 40 stores has its own unique look. According to their president, Glen Senk, they are creating these environments with one kind of customer—and only one—in mind. "Most stores cater to a broad base of customers or specialize in a product category. We specialize in one customer. And we offer her everything from clothing to bed linens to furniture to soap."[2] The Anthropologie customers are unapologetically women 30 to 45 years old, with a college education, families or at least partners, a worldly outlook, and a household income of $150,000 to $200,000. (I hope they don't mind if a few of us older and less well-off women enjoy the stores, too.)

Walking into Anthropologie is an immersive experience—so much so, that visits average more than an hour. The stores smell good and are clean and fun to look at. The merchandise is a wonderful mix of old, new, exotic, fun, and useful, so that every time you turn around you see something that you want to look at more closely. A woman can shop for her home, herself, her children, even her husband (the stores include books and toys), and leave feeling as though she has taken a little vacation.

Borders, Upstart Crow, and Barnes & Noble all figured out that having a separate section for children that includes books, toys, story time, and occasional bits of theater and other performances is a great enticement. Combine that with a good cup of coffee and decent music, and it's easy for Mom and the kids to while away the afternoon at the bookstore. Heck, public libraries ought to investigate adding coffee bars to go with the books.[3] It's that attractive. All three stores offer places to sit—a real boon to anyone herding children all day!

Restoration Hardware is a similar shopping experience. The draw here is nostalgia. The idea of taking the kids through and saying, "Oh my gosh, that's the very same pick-up-sticks game I had as a child!" or, "Look at this, Benjamin. Your grandmother had one just like it!" is too much fun. Their stores not only have a sense of history—as in the detailed product descriptions—but also a sense of humor. They encourage touching and opening and closing and trying. Normally in places such as that, I tell my son to keep his hands in his pockets. But a good part of the experience at Restoration comes from the joy of trying it out. I hardly ever leave without something. And again, it's not on my To-Do list.

Other national and regional chains have worked hard to turn their stores into exciting, engaging, immersive experiences. Nike and Warner Bros.—companies whose histories did not feature much retail experience—were two of the first retailers to buy into the concept of retail entertainment in a really big way. But Jordan's Furniture beat everyone to the punch.

In 1987, this previously unassuming little furniture store chain in Avon, Massachusetts, opened its third store, and included among the couches and coffee tables was a MOM experience: the Motion Odyssey Movie ride. That's right, a motion simulator in a furniture store. But Jordan's, owned by brothers Barry and Eliot Tatelman, was just beginning. When they opened their fourth store in Natick, Massachusetts, in 1998, it included a 262-seat, state-of-the-art, IMAX 3D theater and a replica of New Orleans's Bourbon Street. The brothers swear that the theater boosted business by 20 percent. But you don't have to take their word for it. In October 1999, Warren Buffett acquired the four-store, $300 million company and, wisely, left the boys in charge. Jordan's was scheduled to open a fifth store in 2004 in Framingham, Massachusetts, with an IMAX theater attached to a restaurant, among other things.

What the Tatelman brothers have done for almost 20 years is provide the great service and selection that their father insisted on (he opened the first Jordan's in 1928) and create a niche for themselves that welcomes families with open arms. Jordan's never has sales; instead, it offers year-round low prices. The company really supports its communities, in part by allowing the theaters to be used for various fundraisers—much more fun than a bake sale! If you have to shop for furniture—and most of us do several times over our lifetimes—why not go to the store that makes everyone happy? The kids aren't bored to tears, or screaming and crying while you are trying to pick out a chest-of-drawers for your guest room. They're in the MOM theater having a blast or watching a documentary on elephants in the IMAX theater! The way Jordan's has created its niche is very unconventional, but the results are phenomenal. Perhaps Warner Bros. and Nike had such results in mind when they opened their experiential stores.

Those establishments started springing up in major urban areas in 1990 and made headlines everywhere. The stores became destinations within destinations. People lined up to get into a Niketown, as they would have done to see their favorite rock band at a record store. Once every 20 minutes or so, they got to watch a movie pushing Nike's products and philosophy, among other media extravaganzas. This was as much about brand entertainment as shoes. By 2003, there were 13 Niketowns. They have done particularly well in high-tourism areas, and I'm sure the number of tourists influenced the choice of locations far more than the number of Moms. What Nike did for Moms and the ever-expanding feet of their children was open 74 outlet stores.

Warner Bros. stores were big, bold cartoons come to life, and they sold everything Warner Bros.—clothes, bags, books, animation art, toys, videos, music, games. All the Warner stores included a mini–video theater running Warner cartoons and movie trailers. They even installed interactives for the kids. But by the dawn of the new century, all the Warner Bros. stores were closed. I have a theory about why those stores, and later the Disney stores, never performed to expectations. The choice of what to buy in a store devoted to media depends on some kind of emotional connection to those media—cartoon, movie, song, whatever. Those highly branded media products are, after all, souvenirs. If the retail location itself offers no story or experience to remember (souvenir in French means "to remember"), then the incentive to buy is very low.

Jordan's embraced entertainment with considerably more success than either Nike or Warner Bros. for two main reasons. First, the Jordan's entertainment experience is customer-directed, designed to answer the question, "What would make our customers happy to come?" rather than, "With what brand message do we want to hammer our customers?" Movies at Jordan's are not extended commercials; they're just fun to watch. The furniture it sells is not plastered exclusively with the Jordan's nameplate; lots of different manufacturers are represented. Second, entertainment is not the main draw. It's just a bonus in a store to which people already love to come, for well-established reasons of quality, service, and selection. Paradoxically, Jordan's succeeded with entertainment, in part, because the company really didn't need it.

Not unexpectedly, some of the most wonderful shopping experiences are in stores that are owned and operated locally—the Mom and Pop venues. They are the very stores whose success can portend the upward mobility of a formerly borderline business district. And they are the stores that move on to the next almost-trendy area when the rents skyrocket and only the Gap and J. Crew can afford them. Still, they can offer exceptional shopping experiences for Moms.

Vroman's is my hometown bookstore. For over a hundred years, this family-owned business has tried to enlighten and inspire residents. It offers what you expect of a modern bookstore—huge selection, almost daily author events, book clubs, beautiful gifts, personal service, and a very nice coffee bar. It also has one of the best collections of children's books anywhere, next to a storytime and play area. The staff is so knowledgeable (it's clear they all do read!) that I can go in not knowing the author or the name of the book, only vague plot points, and they can still direct me to what I'm looking for! In addition, the store has a community program called Vroman's Gives Back. If you sign up, 1 percent of your purchases goes into a fund that is divided among 16 local charities—many involving literacy and children. Of course I don't scorn the national booksellers, but given a little bit of time to invest, I'm much more likely to go to Vroman's, because I can turn my son loose and browse for an hour or more and—most important—feel good about the money I spend. Not only is it satisfying my wants, but it's also helping my community.

Another really Mom-friendly place in southern California is the Farmer's Market on Fairfax Avenue, next to The Grove. The Farmer's Market turned 70 in 2004 and, like other well-established markets across the country (such as Reading Terminal Market in Philadelphia), offers something for everyone. Getting lost in its warren of stores can be such an immersive experience that you forget where you came in. The most wonderful thing about the Farmer's Market is its authenticity— it's a slice of real life. Some folks have been meeting their friends there since the place opened. TV executives from nearby CBS grab coffee and a nosh. There are punks with Statue of Liberty spikes and busloads of the ladies of the Red Hat Society. Kids love shopping at the Farmer's Market because *somebody* has *something* cool within their budget. There are probably too many T-shirt and souvenir shops, but even that's part of the charm. Those stores, mixed in with meat markets and bakeries and produce and all kinds of food stands, mean that you can find something for every picky wearer and eater in your household. The seating is communal, unless you actually go into one of the restaurants. It's chaotic and fun. The old people smile and cluck over the young people. The young people nod to the old people and give them the high sign. It is the kind of Town Square experience that developers all over the country are trying to re-create. But this is the real deal. This is an authentic, engaging piece of living history and a great place to get away from it all for a little while.

Finally, alas, one of my favorite places to shop with children is no more. It was a locally owned pet store called Pet Metro. It was a fabulous idea, I thought. The store was divided into environments: one for birds, one for reptiles, one for fish, and one for cats and dogs. You could also find rabbits, hamsters, rats, mice, and guinea pigs scattered about. Within each environment, there were opportunities to interact with the creatures. The fish area had a tidal pool where the kids could touch starfish and anemones and watch crabs scurry from rock to rock. In the reptile section, there were beautifully designed habitats and trained employees who would let you touch a snake, if you were brave enough. The birds had their own separate glass-enclosed room. You could go in and talk to them and pet them. It was both a shopping and a learning experience. But PetCo bought it, and now it's just like every other PetCo nationwide. I can't blame the owners for following the path of the American dream—but I do miss their personal philosophy in this store.

What seems to stick out in all these fun shopping experiences is the overall feeling of being transported to another place, even if it's only for a short time. We Moms are emotional creatures. When my best friend Judy was pregnant with her first-born, she couldn't watch *Bambi*. It just made her bawl. To this day, she can't talk about the scene where Bambi's mother gets killed without choking up. If you can create a place that makes an emotional connection to Mom, caters to her just a little, takes her off her usual treadmill, and welcomes her children, then you are approaching that Disneyland feeling of an authentic and memorable experience. Moreover, not coincidentally, research suggests that brands that engage people emotionally can command prices 20 percent to 200 percent higher than those of competitors and can sell in far higher volumes.[4]

Mom's Circle of Influence

Moms spend a lot of time shopping. My research shows that they go shopping in a place such as Target or Wal-Mart every two weeks or so. Remember, this is To-Do shopping that *must* be done. A very large chunk of it is by and for teenagers. I don't think I'd get much of an argument if I said Moms control almost all shopping decisions for the 0-to-12 age group. Teens, on the other hand, are a totally independent and self-sufficient group, if you listen to the marketing mavens.

Yes, in the year 2000, teenagers spent $105 billion of "their own money" and an additional $50 billion of their parents' money on stuff, according to Teenage Research Unlimited, a market research firm.[5] *But excuse me, how many teenagers do you know who get all their money from outside work? Most states won't even allow them to work until they are 16!* Where are they getting most of this money? I'll tell you where—from me, and the millions of Moms just like me. Based on Teenage Research's own findings, it's reasonable to assume that well over half of teens' "own money" originally came from us parents. So, if teens are spending that much of Mom's money on a yearly basis, the real question is, "Does Mom have any influence on how that money is spent?" You bet she does.

The influence comes in different packages. Moms are the primary source of transportation, as well as funding, for teenage shopping trips. So even if I turn my son loose to buy his own clothes, I have control over *where* he spends his/my money, at least until he can drive. Second, even if I am not right there when he buys a pair of jeans or a T-shirt, I've spent the last ten or so years of his life teaching him *how* to shop, if only indirectly. I've taught him things such as, "You're growing fast; don't spend all your money on something you will outgrow in three months." I've taught him to compare prices. I've taught him to look at the back of the store for the sale rack. These facts escape market researchers because they are hard to quantify; yet they are part and parcel of Mom's circle of influence.

This circle can stretch across both space and time. For instance, how Mom shops is influenced by how *her own* mother shopped. Three-quarters of the Moms in my survey reported that *their* mothers had at least moderate influence on their own shopping. Millions of us buy Tupperware because Mom did. Or we buy Frigidaire appliances because Mom did. Or we buy Tide because Mom did. I know that I didn't have the nerve to switch from Tide to some other clothes detergent until after my mother died. I was afraid of what she'd say if she found out I was using something different. Think for a minute about the possible implications of such influence. It seems to me that if your Mom always took you to the ocean for summer vacation, you are more likely to try to do the same with your own children because, well, it's a tradition, and Moms are the custodians of most family traditions. If your Mom was a real movie hound and dragged you with her, then you are more likely to take your own children to the movies frequently. If your mother loved baseball, as mine did, then you are more likely to take your family to a Major League Baseball game, and that influence has a good chance of continuing after your children reach adulthood, thus increasing the circle of influence.

It doesn't always work so felicitously. When I asked a good friend how her mother had influenced her shopping, she hesitated, smiled ruefully, and said, "She taught me what kind of gin to buy." And yet negative influence is influence, too. Some of us buy things that our mothers would never let us have, such as cookies or ice cream or high-heeled shoes. Others of us go to movies because our mothers forbade it. Or we let our children have coffee because our mothers told us it would stunt our growth. So, a mother's influence is pervasive even if it drives us in the opposite direction. Scary, isn't it?

Moms also influence what teenagers buy. My teen might go to the mall and pick out new shoes for school, plus some socks and underwear. That's not his idea of shopping. It's mine. His idea of shopping is buying a pair of pants covered in zippers and spikes or a new T-shirt with a bit of confrontational wisdom printed on it. He would never say, "Hey, Mom. Can I go sock shopping?" I might not be involved in the final style choice—whether it's socks, underwear, or T-shirts—but it is quite likely that I will suggest or at least approve the purchase before it is made.

Finally, Moms have a lot of influence over how their teenagers shop because they go with them. It's clear that fashion retailers have recognized just how often Moms shop with their teen girls because they have started to carry similar fashions in Mom's size. It seems many Moms want to look like their daughters. The fashions displayed all over retail spaces in 2003 included many styles straight from the 1970s. We had low-riding, hip-hugging jeans with huge belts, midriff-baring tops, and romantic peasant-type blouses that were made out of prints that screamed "Make Love, Not War." I'm sure many mothers still have some of those things in their closets. Naturally, everyone is now embracing the return to the 1980s. Oh joy. Remember yuppies, DINKs, Gray Panthers, and empty nesters? Stand by, because a return to the 1940s is next. You read it here first.

I shop with my son, although it's never occurred to me to dress like him. I try to let him determine his own style, but, even though I rarely use it, I still do have veto power. Among the women with older children in my pilot survey, nine out of ten were involved in the final decision when the kids were shopping for clothes.

In appealing at least in part to Moms, then, far-sighted retailers can substantially improve their sales both now and in years to come. Remember that those billions of dollars spent by teens are influenced, if not directly controlled, by me. Making me—the Mom who controls the money—happy will make you, the retailer, happy.

Customer Service

Customer service deserves an entire book of its own, I think. No other term turned up more often in my survey than customer service—not just in retail, but in restaurants and attractions and every other venue where Moms spend money. The lack of it is not new, and I guess that's what really bugs me. If everybody knows its value and wants it as part of the shopping experience, why is it so hard to find? Time and time again, respondents recalled asking a clerk for help and getting exactly the same response I did from the manager and salesperson at that sporting goods store—"I don't know." Those three little words are often accompanied by attitude, usually one that indicates that I, the customer who makes it possible for them to get paid, have interrupted them. Those three little words are hardly ever followed by the magic words, ". . . but I'll find someone who does." The clerk usually just disappears or manages to make me disappear.

Included in what I call this customer disservice ethic is the idea that I, the Mom, work at the store. If there is no tag on my item, then I am expected to go find one like it. Or if I mention that I've forgotten to pick up a gallon of milk, the response is usually, "If you hurry, I can hold this other stuff for you." I have already taken over many of their tasks. I am responsible for running my credit card or bank card. I am responsible for unloading my cart. I am often responsible for bagging my items. I do my own carryout. In some stores, I even scan my own merchandise. Customers really ask very little of store employees at this point. So I refuse to do their few remaining jobs for them. Of course, in the end, I'm the loser. I have to go somewhere else to get the milk.

An interesting customer service revolution has taken place in the last few years. But don't be surprised if you haven't noticed. By this time, no doubt everyone in the business world has heard the term one-to-one marketing. Don Peppers and Martha Rogers, Ph.D., originators of the term, define it:

> *Focused on the individual customer, one-to-one marketing is based on the idea of an enterprise knowing its customer. Through interactions with that customer, the enterprise can learn how he or she wants to be treated. The enterprise is then able to treat this customer differently than other customers. However, one-to-one marketing does not mean that every single customer needs to be treated uniquely; rather, it means that each customer has a direct input into the way the enterprise behaves with respect to him or her.*[6]

It's a sound philosophy, but with all the attention being paid to customer relations management (CRM) and one-to-one marketing these days—books, newsletters, software, white papers, and endless seminars abound—why don't I, the lowly customer, feel the effects of this new philosophy more profoundly? The techniques preached by Peppers and Rogers really boil down to some old-fashioned common-sense business practices. Take my dry cleaner, for instance.

When I moved to a new neighborhood nine years ago, I took my cleaning to several different establishments before I settled on one. I got satisfactory cleaning from each one, but at Champion Cleaners I got a shock. First of all, they accepted my check and did not ask for my ID; after the third visit, they called me by name. And they still do. It's a family-owned business run by Coco, who speaks four languages, maybe more. He never forgets a face and even more remarkably, he never forgets a garment. He always treats me as though I'm important to his business and as though he cares about me. His employees, some of whom are family members, are carrying on his customer service philosophy. It's an unbeatable combination and a great shopping experience. As long as Coco is in business, he will get mine.

On the other end of the customer service spectrum is my huge chain grocery store. Vons Market, a Safeway company, has been collecting data on me via my Vons card for six or seven years. It knows every product I buy and how often. It knows whether I eat cereal or bagels for breakfast. It knows how many thousands of dollars a year I spend in its store. It knows more about me than my own mother did. And yet, instead of rewarding me at the cash register at the time of purchase, my "reward" from Vons is a bunch of coupons that I have to remember to bring in if I want to take advantage of my "special savings." Or a card I have to remember to get stamped in order to take advantage of "special savings." Or a cash register receipt with a list of limited-time offers that I have to remember to buy next time, in order to take advantage of "special savings." Think what a lovely experience it would be for the cashier to say, "You qualify for an additional 5 percent off your bill today. Thanks for shopping with us." I shopped at Vons mainly for the convenience of its location. But I have slowly pulled away and do more of my shopping in specialty stores, where I am a valued customer.

Even Coco could appreciate another huge company that collects similar customer information, but uses it better. A couple of years ago, Blockbuster, the national video store, started issuing reward cards for $10. The savings were immediate. As soon as you bought the card, you received a free rental. Blockbuster does exactly what Vons doesn't. When I gather up my movies and go to the cashier, he or she will tell me, "You qualify for a free rental. Would you like to use it now?" Or the cashier tells me that I can rent a video game for my son for free. Or *something*. Just about every cash register encounter turns out to have a pleasant surprise waiting for me. I love it! I don't have to remember to do anything except be a loyal customer, and I get lots of positive reinforcement. In addition, Blockbuster sends me coupons in the mail, and, occasionally, there's a special offer on the receipt. But I don't get mad when I forget those things because I'm rewarded anyway. That's how all customer data should be used—to make me feel as though I am of value to the store and to enhance my shopping experience. Otherwise, it's clear that data collection in the name of customer service is a sham—not unlike the old bait and switch—and only for the benefit of stockholders.

Coco knows all this and he doesn't own a computer. He keeps everything and everybody in his head. Vons has all the wonders of modern technology at its fingertips and doesn't know how to use them effectively. Blockbuster has the same technological advantage and has figured out how to use it. The lesson is quite simple: Good customer experiences result in customer loyalty and that all-important word of mouth.

I don't think good customer service is rocket science. It starts at the top and trickles down. The management team sets the priorities. At Vons, management's priorities include limiting the number of bags used per grocery order. Managers decided that if they cut back on the use of bags, then they could save money. So clerks stopped bagging my milk, my paper towels, my toilet paper, or my bag of ice unless I remembered to ask. Here I am again, doing work for the company. It's no problem for the bagger. He lifts the item from the counter into the waiting basket. But I have to get out to the car, into the car, and into my kitchen. If he doesn't bag everything, then it takes me many more trips to clear out the car because I can manage only one milk carton per hand, while I could have managed three bags per hand at a time. That bagger is also the guy who will put 15 pounds of groceries into a single bag and expect me to make it into the house before the bottom falls out. This is a perfect example of a company making me work too hard with nothing to show for it. That's why I'm shopping more and more at Trader Joe's, a specialty chain that tells its employees that packing a bag is an art form. Vons gets my dollars only when I'm in a big hurry and it is the closest grocery. And the change in my attitude is mostly because of lousy customer service.

The irony of this story is that Vons apparently wants to improve customer service. In mid-2002, everyone in all the stores must have been required to attend training sessions. Suddenly, on every trip, I was inundated with employees greeting me and asking me if I was finding everything all right. Everyone said exactly the same thing, per the script. But they weren't interested in real customer service. They were interested in meeting corporate goals. It was so phony, all it did was annoy me. The manager at one store asked me five times during a single visit if I was finding everything. I wasn't and I told him what I needed. What? Good heavens, that kind of customer response was not covered in the script! He never offered to look, to check with his buyers, to write down the items I was looking for—nothing. That is not customer service. It is customer irritation.

The important thing to remember here is that, while it's true that the bottom line for Target, Wal-Mart, and Vons probably doesn't suffer much because of poor customer service, the bottom line could be positively affected if the customer service were better. Increasing the quality of customer service is one way to get and keep customers over time, even if your store is on the To-Do end of the shopping continuum. Customer service training should be looked on as an investment, not as a one-time marketing expense.

End of Customer Service Song-and-Dance Number 302.

Listen to Your Mother

If you are serious about improving your relationship with my money and me, there are some things you can do:

■ If nothing else, improve customer service. This works across the board—even in stores where Mom doesn't expect much.

■ Offer value: a solid balance of quality, price, and selection.

■ Make it easy for Mom to get there and to get around.

■ Welcome the children.

■ Give Mom a fun retreat from hassles of the day. And give her permission to indulge herself.

■ Don't add entertainment unless the shopping experience is already a good one. And think about what Mom will like, not just about what you want to say.

■ Give back to the community.

■ Provide a positive and memorable experience, if you can manage it.

■ Acknowledge that Mom's influence stretches far and wide and make sure she knows you know.

Endnotes

1. Travel Industry Association of America, "The Shopping Traveler," reported by ABCNews.com.

2. Polly LeBarre, "Sophisticated Sell," *Fast Company*, December 2002.

3. The Pasadena Public Library in Pasadena, California, does have a coffee bar on its patio.

4. Linda Tischler, "How Do I Love Thee? Let me Plot the Graph." *Fast Company*, Issue 84, July 2004, p. 64.

5. According to Teenage Research Unlimited, teenagers get their money from the following sources:
• 47 percent from parents on an as-needed basis
• 41 percent from odd jobs
• 41 percent from gifts
• 28 percent from part-time jobs
• 25 percent from regular allowance
• 11 percent from full-time jobs.
Categories total more than 100 percent because many teens get money from multiple sources. I assume that parents are providing all the regular allowance and "as-needed" money, and that they are the source of most odd-job and gift money as well. In other words, that's my money those teens are spending! Teenage Research Unlimited Press Release, January 25, 2001.

6. www.1to1.com, Peppers and Rogers Web site glossary.

Chapter 2

The Highs and Lows
of Mall Fever

don't know whether it's a blessing or a curse to have one's life parallel the
history of the shopping mall in America. I was born in 1953. The first
enclosed mall was Southdale Center built in 1956 in Edina, Minnesota, near
Minneapolis. Modern shopping life hasn't really been the same for either of us since.
The roots of the mall, of course, are in the market fairs that have been held in the
western world at least since William the Conqueror's time. Merchants and buyers
would meet in certain cities at certain times of year—maybe after the wool clip—not
only to do business with other businessmen, but also to sell their wares to the locals.
The fairs often included entertainment such as traveling musicians, acrobats, and
dramatic players. There was food and drink aplenty. It sounds so familiar. Our shopping roots run very deep, but instead of shopping twice a year, we are more likely to
do it twice a month. And when we shop, we often wind up in a shopping center or
mall—a place where all manner of retailers gather to offer their goods. But it's not
just shoes, clothes, and furniture anymore. Increasingly, one finds housing, grocery
stores, doctor's offices, gyms, and more. Shopping centers, in a way, have become
their own little villages.

Do you remember your first mall? I do. I grew up in Amarillo, Texas—population 125,000—where, in 1961, a new shopping marvel called Sunset Center opened. The enclosed mall drew an audience from all over the Texas Panhandle. In typical mall fashion, it was anchored by large department stores and national chains: Penney's, Zale's, Woolworth's, and even Mode O'Day (only your hairstylist knows if you are old enough to remember that chain). Some locals saw it as an evil interloper. My husband's family had always spent their money downtown, or at Wolflin Village, a suburban shopping center close to where the moneyed sort were moving. The stores in Wolflin Village were branches of the downtown stores in many cases, owned by local merchants. There was a lot to be said for buying from someone you knew: White and Kirk, Colbert's Harry Holland, Blackburn Bros., and Circle N Appliance. It wasn't long, though, before my husband and his Mom discovered that there was a Red Goose shoe store at the new mall, and his family, along with those of his friends, widened their shopping circle for a time.

Remember Red Goose shoes? After you bought a new pair of shoes, you could pull the neck on the huge red goose and it would "lay an egg" full of candy and tiny toys.

I mention Sunset Center and Wolflin Village because they illustrate the rollercoaster career of the shopping center in such graphic terms. The mall came to town, and the downtown stores and most of the local merchants in the shopping village appeared doomed. However, something odd happened along the way. Downtown indeed continued its downward spiral, before morphing into a business, financial, and government district largely devoid of retail. But Sunset Center died, too, after thriving for a while. It came back to life with a different mix of tenants, then died again. It was the village that lived, by attracting some successful regional chains while retaining most of its local character. It survives to this day. We have come full circle, and the shopping village and even some inspired downtowns are replacing the covered mall. Developers today fight hard to find qualified local merchants and restaurateurs to balance the mix of national chains. How did we get here? Let's take a moment to look at the history of the mall in America, and the trends and events that punctuated it.

Four Decades of Malls and Shopping Centers

During the 1960s, shopping malls popped up all over the landscape. It was a time of revolution, and not just in shopping. Women were ditching the complex hairdos of the 1950s and going for simplicity—really short hair or really long hair. We gave up our bobby sox and poodle skirts and put on our minis. We were fighting the

Vietnam War, segregation, and sexism with varying degrees of success. We watched in horror as John and Bobby Kennedy and Martin Luther King were assassinated. We started the Peace Corps, and we went to the moon. The Beatles appeared on Ed Sullivan. Rock 'n' roll ruled and riled. And more and more women moved steadily into the workplace.

According to *Shopping Center World*, by 1972 there were 13,174 centers of all sizes spread out across the United States.[1] By the time I was in high school in the late 1960s, "going to the mall" was something we did. In fact, we could go to a mall anywhere in the country and feel right at home. The cookie-cutter approach to design and to tenanting made malls as indistinguishable from one another as McDonald's or Denny's. Just as with young people everywhere, there was this compulsion to look alike, even while paying lip service to the virtues of difference. Diversity and individuality were still foreign descriptors.

The 1970s simultaneously gave rise to the Me Generation and the Decade of the Woman. Bellbottoms, crop tops, and exposed navels were all the rage—sound familiar? Single motherhood took an upswing partly as a result of the rising number of divorces. We debated the Equal Rights Amendment and lost, and we watched *Charlie's Angels* religiously. We were scandalized and energized by Maude's openness (played to perfection by Bea Arthur) and we all fell in love with Mary Tyler Moore. We watched Archie and Meathead argue over race, religion, sex, and every other taboo on *All in the Family*. The Ramones invaded New York, and punk was born. We fell in love for the first time. Some of us got married. Jimmy Carter was elected and rejected. We had horrible inflation and an energy crisis. The American Dream missed a step. Businesses of all types suffered and malls were no exception. As inflation and interest rates soared, developers looked for ways to stabilize their properties, and their first response was to add gross leasable space. Their hope was that by expanding they could spread out the fixed costs of operations. This is America—bigger is better! Instead, they wound up with lots of empty storefronts.

After the 1970s, developers started to look more carefully at individual properties and to see them, not as part of some huge franchise, but as stand-alone businesses. Each property could have its own look and its own personality—a personality that better reflected the makeup of the community in which it was built. It became clearer that it was important to play to the strengths of the consumer, and the developers emerged from a recession stronger and wealthier.

Between 1980 and 1990 we saw the launch of CNN, PacMan and IBM PCs. Sandra Day O'Connor became the first woman appointed to the Supreme Court.

We watched Charles and Diana marry, and before the decade ended, we watched their marriage fall apart. We decided we wanted our MTV! CDs outsold vinyl, and we learned from Bobby McFerrin and Prozac, "Don't worry, be happy." Many of us had children and attended our first PTA meetings and shopped our first back-to-school sales.

In this same decade, we also added another 16,000 shopping centers, for a total of some 36,500 by 1990. Unfortunately, the growth was driven by the availability of capital more than by need. Eventually, this bubble burst, too, and many developers scrambled to downsize projects or convert them to smaller neighborhood or community-centered destinations. Others started to move toward so-called "power centers" with "big box" tenants, referring to shopping centers full of huge mega-stores such as Bed, Bath & Beyond and Best Buy. It was during this time that the department stores—long the steadfast anchors of all forms of malls—got into trouble. There were mergers and bankruptcies that affected almost every single national department store. (Local stores, too: Colbert's went under back in Amarillo, after trying to expand too fast.) Their troubles opened the way for the giant stand-alone discounters like Wal-Mart and Target.

It was also during the 1980s that we saw the flowering of the food court. Fast food was already a necessary accoutrement to our busy, urban lifestyle. And it became a strong moneymaker in the malls. Food courts moved out of the unused corners and took the spotlight, often generating more sales per square foot than the anchors.

Food had rescued the malls for the moment, but another downturn in the early 1990s found cutbacks, poor stock performance, and overbuilding. Innovation wasn't widely acclaimed. Lenders in the 1990s were demanding that new projects have certain highly bankable anchors, and that meant that once again the cookie-cutters were winning. Every mall felt like every other mall. Shoppers were not excited. Developers wanted a magic bullet. All they knew for certain was that, regardless of what happened, we would shop our way through it. They decided that it was their job to make that experience begin to meet desires, not just needs. They had added food and movie theaters. The next step, of course, was to add more entertainment.

If you're going to do it, you might as well do it bigger and bolder. The Ghermezian Bros., Simon and Associates, Teachers Insurance and Annuity Association, and Triple Five Group formed a partnership and rode the crest of the wave toward revitalizing retail with entertainment. Their proof of concept was (and is) the Mall of America. Since it opened its doors in 1992 with more than 300 stores, it has taken shopping to new heights. Today:

■ It has 520 stores.

■ It employs more than 11,000 people.

■ It is 98 percent leased.

■ Total traffic has ranged from 35 to 42 million visits yearly.

■ Visitors spend an average of nearly three hours in the Mall, which is twice the current national average for shopping malls.

■ Mall of America is one of the most visited destinations in the United States, attracting more visitors annually than Disney World, Graceland, and the Grand Canyon combined.[2]

Entertainment at Mall of America includes attractions such as the Camp Snoopy Theme Park, the Underwater Adventure aquarium, General Mills' Cereal Adventure, Jillian's Hi Life Lanes, NASCAR Silicon Motor Speedway, America Live (four nightclubs in one), and an AMC 14-screen theater. There are 45 eateries of various sorts, and the events list includes Toddler Tuesdays for the stroller set, book signings, famous NASCAR drivers giving out autographs, and even special fashion events for teens. Mall of America has a partnership with Northwest Airlines that includes airfare and hotel from most major and many minor cities in the United States and beyond. In short, it represents the pinnacle of the entertainment/shopping destination attraction. And after more than ten years, it seems to get better and better.

Whose Money Is It, Anyway?

Developers and retailers have seen the market drivers change mood and colors so many times over the last 40 years, it has been hard to keep up with the economics of shopping centers. All of them have had to learn marketing skills, diplomacy skills (for dealing with those pesky neighborhood groups), public speaking skills (for presentations to mayors and city councils), and financial magic skills because today's malls can't be "malls." People don't want one in their neighborhood, and no developer wants to build one. A mall has about as much cachet as a themed restaurant. Today's bet is on "lifestyle centers" and/or "mixed-use projects." They are more likely to be open-air, town square–type places that include housing and other amenities: doctor offices, pharmacies, grocery stores, community space, dry cleaners, and health clubs, along with retail, restaurants, and entertainment. The mantra: Let consumers guide decisions.

Fine, but who are those consumers? Traditionally, retailers segment the market by age, and then focus virtually all their attention on youth and young adults. But looking at the market that way is problematic. For example, the number of young adults between 18 and 34 shrank during the 1990s, and the number between 25 and 44 is shrinking in the first decade of this century. In contrast, the number of Americans between 45 and 64 will rise by 16 million between 2001 and 2010, and their annual spending by 2010 will approach $2 trillion, fully one-third more than that of 18-to-39-year-olds.[3] If you aim according to age these days, then it seems to me that your target should shift to the over-44 crowd. But I'm here to suggest a simpler way to follow the money: Target Moms, because Moms control the vast majority of those wallets, regardless of age!

Developers who ignore that do so at their own peril. We, the Mom crowd, have the money. We have the inclination. But mall department stores don't encourage us to spend time or money with them. I went shopping recently at a series (three, to be exact) of national department stores in an attempt to find a dress that was classically styled and appropriate for my age. *Hah!* Everything in every store looked like it was designed for a teenager. The racks were full of clothes inspired by the 1970s. I wore those styles then, but I've changed a bit since high school (I know you haven't, but I have!), and I'm not interested in paisley prints, peasant tops, or lace-up dresses. So I didn't buy a dress. And that's what many other women my age are doing everywhere. We are shopping less even though we have more to spend.

It doesn't matter whether it's sports, politics, or retail—follow the money.

Two characteristics largely determine the attractiveness to Moms of any shopping center: the context, or architectural setting, and the content, or the goods and services available within that setting. One cannot save the other, but each must support the other. It is vital that they work together to provide a shopping experience that is worth repeating. Some developers really understand this and some don't. I am not saying that every shopping or lifestyle center has to cater solely to Moms. That isn't at all necessary. But every shopping center has to have a really good idea to whom it is catering and follow through. The Stanford Shopping Center in Palo Alto, California, clearly is catering to the affluent college students at Stanford, but also to those students' Moms. And it is beautiful. It calls itself a "shopping center disguised as a park." The plantings are scheduled twice a year so that even the gardens invite a repeat visit to see what's new.

Westfield Shoppingtowns, a growing chain of branded malls, is starting to include family lounges as an extra incentive for Moms with small children. These areas offer private nursing stations, baby changing stations, bottle warmers, child-size bathrooms, and sink facilities, a microwave for warming baby's food and bottle, and a comfortable rest area featuring children's movies.

General Growth Properties, the nation's second-largest mall owner/developer, is introducing Club NOGGIN, a new interactive educational experience for young children at five of their malls. Club NOGGIN invites parents and caregivers to bring their young children (three to six years old) to the mall where—for a free 75 minutes—kids can play educational games and participate in large- and small-group activities supervised by trained activity leaders. NOGGIN, a division of Nickleodeon devoted to preschoolers, has created a safe and educational format for the clubs that complements the network's curricular framework and on-air programming. Each club session will include interactive songs, video clips, games, and hands-on activity stations. This is a drop-off program, freeing Mom's hands for an entire hour of less stressful shopping.

Other malls have devised programs that cater to children from birth to 12. For instance, The Mills Corporation has developed Mugsy's Meadow, a free program for kids, but each child must be accompanied by an adult. Wannado City is a theme-park-in-a-mall that is also slated for Mills properties. The first Wannado City has opened at Sawgrass Mills in Sunrise, Florida. Admission is $24.95 for children three to 14 years old. But, like the Camp Snoopy Theme Park in the middle of Mall of America, I see these types of attractions as entertainment options, not shopping enhancements, in part because accompanying the little ones actually takes Mom away from shopping. And it's unlikely Mom has "buy new towels and new shoes" and "take kids to theme park" all on one To-Do list.

So if you are a mall, you need to be able to answer the question, "Who do you want to be when you grow up?" Do you want to be a family place? Do you want to attract the money of the gray-haired set? Do you want only chic 20-somethings? Do you want to be all things to all people? It's important to focus on your market, whatever it is—not just in the architectural context but also in the content, the tenants that populate these centers. Shaheen Sadeghi proves the point.

The Antimall

Only California could give birth to the mall that is not a mall. And maybe only in California could a man launch the idea with such incredible success. Sadeghi breaks all the rules, and yet he understands the interplay of content and context better than anyone I know. The antimall, his brainchild, is called The LAB. Built in 1993, it is located in Costa Mesa right across from its younger sibling, The CAMP (built in 2002), and on the drawing boards is a third shopping venue designed for mothers and young children.

Before Sadeghi became a developer, he was president of Quiksilver, a billion-dollar apparel company that caters to the board set: surfboards, skateboards, snow-boards, and all the extreme variations. It was during his tenure there that Sadeghi found the key to cool. He discovered that when Quiksilver clothes went into the ail-ing department stores, the brand saw a decline in cool. The kids who wore the clothes wanted authenticity (there it is again) and they wanted something that was their own, not something that had sold out to the establishment.

With this lesson in mind, Sadeghi left the world of apparel to become a real estate developer, and, in the process, gave his old customer base a space of its own. Not only can the young, urban chic find their kind of clothes and accessories and eateries, they find these things in a setting designed to appeal particularly to them. With the creative assistance of designer Ron Pompei (who also designs for Urban Outfitters and Anthropologie), Sadeghi turned a 40,000-square-foot night-goggle factory into The LAB, the antithesis of the local mall. It began with a core of 17 stores and restaurants. Many of them had never had a mall presence before, but they were all geared to urban youth. The setting seems to be part political statement, part performance space and part tribute to a generation that normally gets knocked for being in trouble, on edge and cynical. Across the street, The CAMP appeals to a dif-ferent group just as effectively. It includes a pool for testing and learning about scuba gear, a yoga studio, a health food/fast-food restaurant, and an amphitheater; the landscaping is all done with indigenous vegetation.

I have visited both The LAB and The CAMP, and while I readily admit there's not much for a 50-something mother to buy for herself, I liked them. They weren't built or tenanted for me, but that didn't seem to matter to the conscientious employ-ees of the various stores. I got no attitude or condescending looks. I found that no matter what store I went into at The LAB, I was treated like one of the in crowd—just as if I, too, had tattoos and nose rings! In fact, a young man at Urban Outfitters, the antimall's anchor, who was covered in tattoos and piercings, was one of the nicest store clerks I've ever met. I just kept telling myself that he was some mother's son, and she certainly did raise a polite boy.

I asked Sadeghi if he is involved in his tenants' customer service practices. He replied, "Absolutely. I have to be." It seemed clear to me that he was, because across the street at The CAMP—the first-ever concentration of retailers devoted to outdoor sports—I found the same degree of customer service. In fact, in the Billabong store, I spent a hundred bucks (unplanned) in part because I found the help so responsive. The level of customer service was compelling—so much so that I probably would go back to shop for my son, even though it's at least an hour drive for me.

Customer Service, Again

Customer service is such a big part of creating an ongoing relationship with customers. We all crave it and yet we rarely experience really great customer service. In Chapter 1, I wrote an entire section on the horrors of modern customer service, but just to give you hope, let me recount a counterexample in which I found the service to be exceptional. A couple of friends of mine got married, and in so doing combined families to have six kids. I was trying to come up with a clever wedding present for them and thought it would be fun to get them a series of movies that featured large families. I found myself in Sam Goody's at the local mall thumbing through dozens of DVDs and not finding much. One of the clerks—a young woman with gothic black hair and red lips and dozens of piercings—approached and asked if she could help me. I said yes, and *then* looked up at her. Stifling a gasp (I admit that I have a problem with the current fads in body art, but I also know it's *my* problem), I told her my idea. She thought it was great and started making suggestions. We had a great time picking things out, but the most amazing moment was when she was stumped for a movie title. She excused herself for a minute and came back all excited. "I called my mom and she remembered the name: it was *With Six You Get Eggroll.*" Now tell me, how often does a clerk consult her mother in an effort to help you? She was great and I spent $75 on movies. We all were winners. Yet at the same mall, I can spend half an hour at one of the large anchor stores on a slow day and never encounter a salesperson—or else I'll find one who makes it clear that I am interrupting his *real* job.

This is a big, fat, juicy hint to all developers and to all retailers—I don't care how employees look, I just want them to be nice and helpful. Is that asking too much?

The whole idea of good customer service will raise its noble head throughout this book. But when we are talking about malls and shopping centers, it is especially important and too often ignored. When developers build a project, they either open an in-house leasing office or work with brokers to rent the spaces. They make their money in a variety of ways. Revenue comes from base rents and sometimes from the performance of the retailer within that space; in other words, the developer can take a percentage of the per-square-foot gross sales. In either case, the developer's success is tied directly to the success of the tenant. In the past, the emphasis on the developer's relationship with tenants has been on what they could do to the physical space: the facade, the lighting, the window presentations. Less attention has been paid to the importance of customer service in building clientele, and, I believe, there's even a certain reluctance to interfere with the employer/employee relationship on the part of the developer. That can change. Shaheen Sadeghi has proved that active involvement in customer service is a win/win situation. Developers set rules and standards for every aspect of the tenancy; it's time for those rules to include basic customer service. Setting the bar high and then enforcing it will benefit everyone's bottom line, not the least, that of the developers. In the process, the customer (aka Mom)—who really wants to be loyal—will be thrilled!

Let me give you a personal and detailed example of the influence of bad customer service, among other things, on the success of a project as a whole. A large national development firm built (but no longer owns) a lifestyle center to replace an old, ugly, dead mall in a medium-sized city. Let's call it the Shops on Main Street. When it was announced, I became a vocal supporter for the idea because I lived in the area it would serve. A street that had been closed off to accommodate the old mall was reopened, and just that simple step led the way in reconnecting downtown visually and practically. I visited the offices of the architects on the project, and loved the drawings I saw; I went to preopening events. I really wanted this project to happen because I felt it would enhance the lifestyle of all residents of the area.

Once grand-opening fever had subsided a bit, I took my family to see the first of the *Lord of the Rings* trilogy there. We, and about six other people, were directed to one of the new theaters with stadium seating, and we sat and sat—and sat. Nothing appeared on the screen, not even the usual slide show. Finally, my husband went to check with someone to see what was wrong. It turns out the ticket-taker had seated us in the wrong theater and the movie was just starting down the hall. Ouch. They did apologize and gave us free passes for some future film. It was a good thing because I might not have returned.

After the movie, we went to the fast-food section of the center and decided on Asian food. We walked into an empty restaurant and stood and looked at the employees behind the counter for almost three minutes before they interrupted their conversation to help us. Then they acted really irritated that they had to wait on us. This is the kind of attitude you often see after a place has been open for several years and everyone is on automatic. But this was the brand-new opening crew. They had supposedly been specially trained, and yet we were so turned off by their attitude that we have never gone back. Maybe I'm an unusually tough customer, but most of the time you get only one chance with me. It seems that the better part of valor would be to assume all customers are like me.

Our next Shops on Main Street experience was not much better. We again tried the theater; after all, we had free passes. This time, halfway through the film, the fire alarm went off. No employee came into the theater to explain. Most of us sat there for a while, assuming it was a false alarm. When no one bothered to tell us what was going on, we got up to leave. Out in the corridor there were about five employees laughing and talking and giggling and telling us to go back and sit down. It was a false alarm. No one ever came in and apologized. No one ever explained what had happened. The result? It took my family six months to get our courage up to try the theater once again. I'll be darned if we didn't have another bad experience. We don't usually eat at the theater, but circumstances dictated that course of action. So we ordered three hotdogs. Well, they weren't ready. They wouldn't be ready for 15 or 20 minutes, but not to worry, someone would bring them to us in our seats. Well, that sounded like a nice way to compensate for whoever failed to start cooking the hot-dogs at the right time. So we seated ourselves in the theater and began the wait. And we waited and waited and saw two or three people come in with hotdogs. That tipped us off that they were ready. So my long-suffering husband went to check it out. Sure enough, those hotdogs we saw walk into the theater were ours, but they had forgotten us and now they had to cook some more!! Double ouch. Now, the only time I go to this theater is if the movie is one I really want to see, it's not show-ing anywhere else, and there's a cheap matinee. That happens rarely. I also avoid spending any more than ticket money there. I don't want to encourage them. I'm permanently mad at them. And I can guarantee you I'm not alone. Moms talk to other Moms about family entertainment experiences. Not only do we talk, we listen and we act on what we hear. I have yet to hear anyone in my circle praise that theater—and it's supposed to be a major draw for the center!

Lessons from the Front

Thus, bad customer service in two separate establishments proved disastrous for this Mom's experience in what ought to be a wonderful new retail environment. But from the Mom perspective, customer service is not the only problem at the Shops on Main Street. It is packed with trendy boutique clothing stores that demand you be 16 to 35 years old and smaller than a size 8. Guess what? There are 47 million women and girls in this country who are size 14 or larger. There are seven stores that supposedly offer apparel for men, but only Eddie Bauer is even partially aimed at my 50-ish husband. Tommy Bahama, Quiksilver and Lucky Brand Dungarees are all geared to a much younger demographic. So already, I can't shop for myself or for my husband. That leaves my son. There are a KB Toys store and a Brookstone. He, of course, can wear the clothes in the so-called men's stores, but he doesn't. He's after

Pac Sun, Hot Topic, Tony Hawk. The Shops on Main Street has recently added a Quiksilver store, but it's not compelling enough to draw this particular teen. So who is the audience for this center? What were they thinking—and what should they have done?

I'm going to go out on a limb here and draw some conclusions using only a few of the many factors that developers, retailers, and financiers should look at in making decisions regarding the building and tenanting of a lifestyle center. I know that it is impossible to base decisions of such magnitude on an analysis this simple-minded, but it is also unwise to ignore the obvious, so bear with me.

Our city has approximately 136,000 people. If I draw a ring five miles out around the Shops on Main Street, then I can include at least four other communities. It is a reasonable assumption that people from these areas would shop in my city and at the Shops on Main Street in particular if their needs were met. So that adds at least another 56,000 people to the mix. The median age in my city and in the state is a little over 35. The median age in the surrounding communities is about 43, with the exception of one where it is 37. It's clear that most of my neighbors and I are older than the usual 18-to-35 target market of most retailers. Census data reveal we are a highly educated group. We own our own homes. We have small families of one or two children, and we have pretty high incomes, with two of the communities bringing the rest of us up considerably. And of course, the majority of us are women. On the face of it, this would seem to be an older, affluent, upscale market just waiting to be tapped. But the tenant mix at the Shops on Main Street skirts this demographic almost completely. Its stores currently include Therapy, Planet Funk, Leather Town, Jaloux/Zalu, Flutter, and Betsey Johnson. For the rest of us, there's J. Jill and Ann Taylor Loft. That's it. Part of the problem here might have been the fact that the original developer put the Shops on Main Street on the market before it opened. That probably caused confusion and uncertainty among the potential tenants and kept some out that might have added balance to the mix. In any case, the center was still not fully leased four years after its November 2000 opening.

Recently, even though one of the three upscale restaurants has closed, the night traffic has picked up considerably. On one summer Saturday night, this center was packed with kids between the ages of about 13 and 18, going to or coming from the movies. But other than the theater, an ice cream store, and that wonderful Asian fast-food I mentioned earlier, there aren't many places for these teens to spend money. Very few of the stores and vendor carts stay open late. So now that the theater is doing its job and attracting huge numbers of people, they seem to be the wrong people for the stores that are there.

The Shops on Main Street's management doesn't even seem to be able to take advantage of the captive audience across the street at the city Convention Center and Auditorium. On the nights we've gone to a symphony performance, we and the rest of the older crowd have found nothing to attract us to the Shops on Main Street afterward. Everything closes up early with the exception of Starbucks, which is in the far corner away from the auditorium—a very long walk in high heels. Most of the stores close at 7:00 p.m. every night. The fast food restaurants are closed by 10:00 p.m.—even if the last movie doesn't get out until much later. As a consumer, I just get confused trying to figure out why I should go to the Shops on Main Street at all, on Saturday night or any other time.

Unfortunately, it's not just the content here that disappoints—it's the context. Designed to feel like a European street, the Shops on Main Street feels more like an American back alley—in spite of the fact that the concept drawings seemed so inviting. There are two levels, but the access to the second level is far from intuitive. The faux street is very narrow and it's difficult to look ahead and figure out what's waiting for you. The sight lines and access need to work for the shoppers, not just look good on paper.

I still want the Shops on Main Street to work. But, right now, it doesn't, not for my family. It is emphatically *not* fun. It can be fixed. Over time, the tenant mix can change to attract Mom as well as tweens Madison and Brittany. The buildings can be repainted to be more inviting and less confusing. The way-finding can improve. The marketing to the captive audience across the street can kick in and give the place some adult energy at night. Customer service could even become the marketing mantra: "Shop at the Shops on Main Street and be treated like the royalty you are." The apartments, which top the complex, can get filled and generate that small-village dynamic. But all this requires a more thorough understanding of the potential customers than the Shops on Main Street has demonstrated so far.

Most shopping is still a necessity, not a luxury (see Chapter 1). But if addressing that necessity can also be engaging or entertaining, and not leave Mom drained and frustrated at the end of the outing, then the developer and the leasing agent and the individual store have won! You can't make Mom choose between a trip to the mall to look at new furniture and going to her daughter's soccer game. She really wants to do both, so help her out! You can't afford to frustrate her by having her spend 20 minutes getting to the information desk because she chose to park near the wrong entrance. Make your conveniences convenient. You can't charge her so much to park that it becomes prohibitive to stop and "run in." She won't stop. You can't attract her if you don't offer her what she *needs* as well as what she *wants*. If you can do all this in a family-friendly setting that is beautiful and stimulating, then not only have you got her, you have her family, her friends, and their collective financial resources.

What Grandma and Grandpa Had

There have been many milestones in the life of the shopping mall. Just like people of a certain age, it keeps trying to discover what's new, what's hip, what works, and what doesn't. The Shops on Main Street doesn't work, for a lot of reasons, even though it was supposed to be a shining exemplar of those new lifestyle centers I mentioned earlier. The driving motivation for building these mixed-use projects is, in part, to recapture what we think our grandparents had. In 1997, I interviewed Mickey Steinberg for an article in *The EZone*. At the time, he had left Disney to help Sony design, develop, and operate Metreon in San Francisco. I loved how he defined the concept of an urban entertainment center (one of the many descriptive terms that have fallen out of use for retail destinations): "Everybody talks about the fact that urban entertainment is a new idea. That's baloney. I was raised in Augusta, Georgia. It was a town of 80,000 and we had the greatest retail entertainment center I ever saw. It was fantastic. We had three department stores, we had four movie theaters, we had bookstores, we had Mom and Pop shops, we had restaurants, we had fast-food restaurants, we had a bowling alley, and we had a pool hall. We called it 'downtown.'"[4]

Many developers of faux town squares like Easton Towne Center in Columbus, Ohio, have taken a cue from the increasingly common and sometimes inspired restoration of our true city centers. It's hard to go through a metropolis of any size and not see a sign directing you to Old Town. Old Town is that series of storefronts that grew up around the original city core. Local governments, historical and heritage groups, and developers have all noticed that, when done right, revitalizing the city core offers something that's hard to come by these days—authenticity.

Easton Towne Center, which opened in 1999, really took the idea of the old-fashioned town square to heart. The outside is designed to look like a town, complete with train depot, high school, library, theater, and other landmarks. But these facades hide traditional retailers such as Barnes & Noble, Pottery Barn, and high-end restaurants. Developer Yaromir Steiner made a conscious effort to combine the allure of a downtown with the convenience of a more traditional mall. In the years since the center opened, an additional 300,000 square feet has been added. The highly successful project boasts a theater company, clubs, bars, a Gameworks, and a Club Libby Lu (where preteen girls can go to get makeovers and feel like teenagers), for a total of 120 tenants. This particular "town center" happens to be on the east side of town, on the loop that goes around Columbus.

New lifestyle centers are in the works all over my neck of the woods and yours, I'm sure. And they are more and more sensitive to the needs of the community—not a looks-good-on-paper community, but the real thing. Community, in fact, is one key to successful projects of this type. The best of them enhance people's sense of their community, by echoing its architecture, conveying its history, or interpreting its story. They provide a geographical, cultural, and psychological center for the people who flock to them, and if they're done well, Moms, in general, find them very cool. Richard Rich, a developer with Millennia Associates, a company associated with the Jerde Partnership, started preaching passionately on the subject of community branding in the late 1990s. "If you do it right and develop a place people think of not as another mall but as 'my place,' then you will win instant acceptance, broad market penetration and repeat visitation—the keys to success in any non-tourist-driven market."[5] A new city center in Rancho Cucamonga, California, will provide proof of his argument, if—unlike the Shops on Main Street—its execution bears out the promise of its design.

Ever since the days of Jack Benny's radio show, this Inland Empire city (then referred to only as *Cu . . . . . . camonga* in Mel Blanc's list of train stops) has been the butt of jokes, but no more. Yesterday's joke is today's golden opportunity. Victoria Gardens, a project directed at the relatively affluent residents who moved to the area because they could get better housing, opened in October 2004. The nouveau downtown, a partnership of Forest City Development California, Inc., and Lewis Investment Co., includes the city's main library, a community theater space, and 400 townhouse apartments, along with national brands that appeal to boomers—bookstores, home improvement stores, home furnishings, restaurants, apparel for the whole family, grocery store, music store, and educational goods store. It is designed to look like a city center that evolved over the years, in keeping with its surroundings, and it is explicitly geared to attract families with children to its greenswards, water features, and other play areas. Moms, I predict, will love both the striving for authenticity and the kid-friendliness.[6]

All over the country, bedroom communities, built decades ago, have evolved into real cities, and now they want a downtown of their very own. Projects like Victoria Gardens can meet that need, but many of the challenges of building a new city center are the same as those of building a mall out on the periphery. Getting the right tenant mix is key. Otherwise all we have done is create malls that just *look* like town centers. It's hard to find tenants that will give a project a unique feel and that financiers will love. That has always been the developers' biggest problem. Even those who think outside the old mall box have to fund their projects. And they normally do that by preleasing to well-known money-making retailers. But if they aren't careful, they get the same well-known money-making retailers that are in the old mall five miles away, and the cookie-cutter has started working all over again.

The Grove, a Caruso project, walks that fine line nicely. It has been very successful, though part of its success can be attributed to the fact that it is built right next to the Farmer's Market, a Los Angeles institution since the 1930s. The Farmer's Market lends the project its air of authenticity. The Grove adds some 40 retailers, a multiplex, and six major restaurants in a setting that is reminiscent of Disneyland's Main Street in its detail. In a speech at the March 2003 ULI conference on entertainment and real estate, Rick Caruso, founder and CEO of Caruso Affiliated, said that The Grove was designed for the shopping wife. Actually, I think he misspoke. Caruso designed it for the shopping Mom. The mixture of retail allows Mom to shop for her whole family in a setting that is delightful and engaging. In the morning, The Grove encourages the stroller-set by offering entertainment for toddlers on the grass in the center of the project. My teenager gave it a very high "cool" score. He loved shopping at all the "board" stores and could have disappeared in the Apple store for hours. He liked the fact that there were a lot of young people hanging out. He said the people-watching was great (translated, I think that means girl-watching). My husband enjoyed the atmosphere, the food, and the fact that he found a couple of shops that he felt were unique. I got to shop at stores that understand me and where I am in my life: Nordstrom, Anthropologie, and Crate & Barrel. We found a new restaurant to try and ate outside. The food was good and the service sincerely nice. Wrap all that together, and The Grove was fun for all of us!

Opportunities to establish more of these community-centered multiuse projects that work for Mom and everybody else exist all across America. They are what PricewaterhouseCoopers calls "greyfields," obsolete regional malls that have around 350,000 square feet of space and annual sales of less than $150 per square foot. The Shops on Main Street was once a greyfield. According to PWC, there are 140 or more bona fide greyfields and 250 headed in that direction in the United States.[7] Although many of these sites no longer have mall potential, they might represent terrific redevelopment options with some combination of housing, retail, office, and community space.

Transformation of the Mall

With all the excitement about revamping greyfields and revitalizing city centers, you might conclude that malls are dead. Not so. Some, like gangly teenagers, have experienced a growth spurt; others, like a fuzzy caterpillar, have undergone a metamorphosis. They have also started to diversify. There's the more traditional mall, such as the ones in my own backyard—Glendale Galleria and Westfield's Shoppingtown Santa Anita. Architecturally, they haven't changed much. They are still inside malls with major anchors, a food court, a theater, and all the major and a few minor national chains. And there are high-end malls such as Fashion Island in Newport Beach and South Coast Plaza in Costa Mesa, featuring top-of-the-marquee stores such as Versace, Armani, Chanel, and Bulgari. But the Mills Corporation (not to be confused with the Mills Brothers) has come up with another concept, and it's taking the country by storm.

Take a look at Ontario Mills, one of 20 eponymous Mills projects across the country. (The Mills Corporation, as of 2003, also had ten other projects under different names, including the entertainment-oriented The Block at Orange in Orange County, California, and Madrid Xanadu, with more projects opening yearly.) The Mills projects tend to be huge covered malls featuring lots of designer outlets and value-priced retailers, lots of entertainment, and lots of food. They attract a younger, less affluent demographic—mainly, I fear, those who have the grit and stamina to last as they make it through the places on their quest for bargains on name brand offerings! The Mills projects emphasize entertainment. You can find large-format theaters and regular movie theaters on their properties, along with GameWorks, Dave and Buster's, or Jillian's. They have their own television network, with monitors all through the properties keeping shoppers updated on what, when, and where things are happening in the mall. Some of the Mills projects have a variety of sports offerings—skate parks or ice rinks—and now they offer at least two different attractions for little kids—Wannado City and Mugsy's Meadow. There's always something going on. If you have children of an age where they can go off on their own and meet you at a predetermined landmark, then a Mills center might be just the ticket. If you are combining shopping with a day of entertainment, then it still sounds like a good bet for most families. If there is a drawback, it's that the places are so huge! Parking and lugging and shopping with small children might be more painful than it's worth.

Redeveloped downtowns; old malls turned inside out; megamalls with an emphasis on entertainment; city centers to create a sense of community; high-end malls for the moneyed; outlet malls for the price-conscious; multiuse malls with housing and grocery stores—it's clear there's no such thing as just a mall anymore. As long as each place can focus on its true core customers, then there's room for everyone—striped caterpillars to golden butterflies. Just don't forget the power of Mom.

Listen to Your Mother

It seems to me that understanding the Mom Factor can help assure success in new projects in all these categories. We have already established that Moms make the buying decisions and the entertainment decisions for their families. We know they can be loyal and that they can influence the buying habits of their families and friends. We know they look for clean, safe spaces to take their families. We know that they are more likely to frequent places that have some sort of connection to their community. The developers and retailers that use a Mom's circle of influence will prosper.

Becoming a mother changes how a woman lives. Mom doesn't necessarily want a *lifestyle*, because she has a *life*. Because she must, she learns early to multitask. Because she must, she learns to schedule and she learns the value of time—the gold of the 21st century. Today, Mom has no time to waste (as if she ever did!). If there's any to spare, she wants to spend it with her family or possibly in a nice hot bath. Remember, anything you do to help Mom conserve her valuable time and restore her flagging energy makes you an angel. For pity's sake, put in enough benches, for she has a long memory for discomfort. Entertaining her and her family is great; engaging them is even better. Listen to her. Cater to her. To gain her loyalty, accept her family as it really exists. Understand that families have grandmas who need to sit down to watch the kids play in the fountain, that they have men who buy plain old pants and shirts (assuming that styles other than islandwear are available), that they sometimes have teenagers *and* toddlers, and that Mom herself works and makes cookies and sometimes even buys pretty dresses for herself. Give her content and a context that are worthy of her time and dollars. If you do it right, your most faithful customer will be Mom.

Endnotes

1. Historical mall numbers and characteristics in this section are based on Brannon Boswell, "Hot Topic: Commemorating 30," *Shopping Center World*, January 1, 2002; and on "NRB Shopping Center Census—18 Year Trends," www.icsc.org/srch/rsrch/census, 2004.

2. www.mallofamerica.com; "Still Heading for the Mall," www.icsc.org, June 2002.

3. David B. Wolfe and Robert Snyder, *Ageless Marketing: Strategies for Reaching the Hearts and Minds of the New Consumer Majority* (Chicago: Dearborn Trade Publishing, 2003), pp. 21–23.

4. *The EZone*, vol. 1, no. 10, July 1997.

5. *The EZone*, vol. 2, no. 6, March 1998.

6. www.ci.rancho-cucamonga.ca.us/victoria/.

7. *Greyfields into Goldfields*. A Study by Congress for the New Urbanism and PricewaterhouseCoopers (San Francisco: Congress for the New Urbanism, February 2001); "Malls: Death of an American Icon," www.money.cnn.com, July 8, 2003.

Chapter 3

I'm Not Cooking Tonight!

When asked where she would take her family out to eat if price and place were no object, my friend Jan from California offered this: Don't laugh, but I would choose a Mennonite/Amish restaurant for true family-friendly dining. There are a number of them in the East and in Florida, and they all offer similar things:

- The food is good, homemade, plentiful, and inexpensive (albeit caloric).
- There are always a good number of tables—with three generations sitting at them—that are helpful to older people as well as children because they accommodate wheelchairs and high chairs.
- They are immaculately clean.
- The service is friendly.

The idea of eating out can probably be traced to some early human who could smell the meat cooking at the fire next door, decided he didn't want to dirty his fire ring, and offered to trade a skinscraper for a dinner. As soon as people started traveling far enough from home to require an overnight stay, then providing a bed and a meal became an entrepreneurial enterprise. An inn with a reputation for the sweetest mead or the most succulent meat, the most responsive service, and the most convivial clientele could do a booming business. Not much has changed in the 1,000-year history of restaurants. Or has it?

The Meal as Experience

I have had the privilege of visiting a medium-sized city in Italy many times on business. I've been there alone, with just my husband, and with both my husband and my son. The three of us even took the grandparents once. And without exception, everyone's most vivid memories are of the wonderful evening meals at a succession of local restaurants. They usually began at 8:00 p.m. and ended as late as midnight. Three to four hours for dinner—every night! Each dish was presented with pride, and each seemed even more delightful than the last. Service was crisp and efficient, but also friendly. There was lots of laughter and talking and sharing, and over those hours, it seemed as though our family grew to encompass the whole room. Sometimes the meal was followed by a stroll and coffee or gelato, but the food and its enjoyment were the centerpiece of the evening.

American equivalents to Italian feasting are increasingly hard to come by these days, and they are less common in restaurants than in the home. Traditional holiday dinners at Christmas, Thanksgiving, and Passover come to mind, of course: several courses and huge portions with an extended family and friends. Where I grew up in Texas, we always had a special Sunday dinner of pot roast or fried chicken. It was the one day during the week when Mom and Dad (he was the real cook in our family) had time to devote to cooking. Often there were guests—aunts, uncles, cousins, friends, airmen from the nearby Air Force base, whomever Daddy could gather up. But even on holidays and Sundays, a meal might have lasted only two hours or so (depending in some cases on when the football game started). Nowadays, though holiday celebrations remain, big Sunday dinners are gone, at least for my family and most of the folks I know. If we do anything similar at all, it's the occasional Sunday brunch. We've gotten so busy that it's often difficult to tell the difference between weekdays and weekends.

Americans are so busy, in fact, that families who actually sit down regularly for meals together at home are much rarer than they used to be. Parents have overscheduled lives and so do the kids. One of the casualties of our speed of life is that food is not often given a chance to be the centerpiece of an experience. It has become merely a means to an end. We eat because the clock tells us that we should, and sometimes we consume an entire meal in minutes. Go on, admit it. You've eaten Pop Tarts on the way out the door in the morning or a Whopper in the car on the way to get the cleaning and do your banking on your "lunch hour." Our children have caught this need-for-speed disease, too. When my son was in elementary school, he would eat his lunch in five minutes or less so that he could play. Playing was much more important than finishing his fruit or his milk.

So if we don't have time to cook a meal and then sit down together and eat it, what do we do? We eat out, naturally.

Eating Out Yesterday

The phenomenon of families eating out is not new, of course, but it used to be a lot less common. My mother worked my whole life. She was a newspaper reporter, proofreader, news editor, magazine editor, and, after she retired, my business partner. She was no cook and never really enjoyed grinding out three meals a day for a family of four, but she felt she had no choice. Until I went off to college, eating out was a big deal at our house. It was reserved for special occasions, not a daily option for lunch or dinner. I remember how exciting it was to go get the Burger Chef ten-for-a-dollar hamburgers on Tuesday nights. Occasionally, we'd go to the only Chinese restaurant in town for egg foo yung and fried rice. The memories are as sweet as the food was pungent. And not just for me. Many of us have very vivid memories of eating out.

My husband's favorite childhood food memory is of the local A&W drive-in in the days of the carhop. He can lovingly describe the root beer delivered to the car in frosty mugs and the icy root beer that clung to the sides and then slid down for slurping. That was entertainment. It was also an event.

Caroline, who grew up in New York City, remembers eating out in Chinatown with her family. "There was a restaurant called Shanghai Village. They had waiters who always remembered us and what we liked, and they trusted me with chopsticks. I *never* used a fork. They served sizzling rice soup that made the noisiest hot rice-crispy crackling sound when the rice was dropped in the boiling soup." She reports that after the great cook and the attentive waiters left, the restaurant vanished.

But Caroline's fondest memory is of La Cave Henry IV. "I ate very garlicky escargot here for the first time. I was seven years old and had to wear a dress and my patent leather shoes. It was in the basement of a building—you had to go down a narrow, short flight of steps, which were decorated to look like a cave. (Aha! A themed restaurant!) Nothing on the menu was written in English. Everything was served with a rich cream sauce and the waiters talked like zees and pulled the chair out for me." The very atmosphere inspired good manners. Eating out was still an occasion, and sometimes a very formal one.

Eating Out Today

Things have certainly changed. Unlike my Mom, I have a choice. I can look at my husband and say, "What do you want for dinner? I'm not cooking tonight." We go out, we order dinners delivered, or we pick up takeout. It happens as many times a week as I can manage it without feeling guilty. (One interesting consequence is that my son almost never wants to go out to eat. He would rather stay home and eat grilled cheese sandwiches. The pendulum never stops swinging.)

Kathy and her husband and two kids are representative of the dining-out experience of today. For them and for many, the family dinner out on the weekend is typically part of the evening's entertainment and not just a meal. So, when they go out, they pick one of the Japanese Teppan restaurants where the food is cooked in front of you. "The food is fresh and everyone likes it. It's a good roundtable setting, and there's lots of interaction with the cook and other people at the table. Kids and adults enjoy it."

In recent years, themed restaurants have taken the idea of dining as entertainment a few steps further. Maybe it's a symptom of our overscheduled lives that we have this desire to cram more than just food into a restaurant meal. We love multitasking! When I began covering the food arena, restaurants such as Planet Hollywood, Rainforest Café, and Hard Rock Café were dominating the news. The imaginative combination of an "experience" accompanied by a hamburger was taking the industry and Wall Street by storm. The idea was that if we could do two things at once—see movie artifacts or learn about the plight of the gorilla while eating—we'd feel great because we hadn't wasted any time. The emphasis was on the experience, and too little attention was paid to food. Animatronic elephants, Elvis Presley's pants and models of the USS Enterprise certainly got diners' attention, but these places soon became tourist curiosities, spots to take Aunt Betty when she was in town. They had trouble with the much-needed repeat local customer, the true heart of a successful eatery. The conclusion from critics and patrons alike was that, for the most part, the food at these places was unremarkable—and how attractive were Elvis's pants on a repeat basis anyway?

I don't want to give you the wrong impression—all three restaurant chains remain profitable and have expanded internationally, in part, because each has reinvented itself. They emphasize food more, and the entertainment has gone beyond mere exhibitry. In fact, no one calls them "themed restaurants" any more—the industry came to regard the term as a jinx after a series of other concepts failed miserably. Now they are "experiential dining choices." All have merchandise lines. Hard Rock has added gaming, both online and off, and Planet Hollywood's Web site is full of the latest news from Hollywood. Like the customers they serve, these companies have gotten more sophisticated, but only Rainforest Café strikes me as a family restaurant. Note, however, that its tagline is "A Wild Place to Shop and Eat"; the fact that shopping comes first is some indication that merchandising is the primary driver here. It does offer educational tours—for a price—that lecture schoolkids about the rainforest, but as near as I can tell, the ticket doesn't include food.

Today, Americans eat out an average of six to nine times a week. The National Restaurant Association predicts that we will spend approximately $124 billion at fast-food restaurants in 2004 and another $158 billion at full-service restaurants. It is estimated that almost half of all American adults patronize a restaurant on any given day.[1] *Half! Every day!*

All of us no doubt would prefer each meal to have the feel of the best Thanksgiving dinners where we are surrounded by family and friends, and served lovingly prepared food. It's just that we now look for someone else to do the loving preparation, clean up the mess, and, in some cases, provide the ambience. We eat out. The only plan I can come up with that would change this scenario is for every mother to have a stay-at-home wife who loves to cook!

A Veggie Burger at Mickey D's?!

Moms still make most meal-planning decisions, especially when it comes to the evening meal. We decide how much time we have between school pickup and soccer. We decide whether it will be pasta or chicken or Baja Fresh or China Wok. We decide whether we will attempt to get everybody to the same table at the same time or settle for rotational seating arrangements because of multiple schedules. We decide if we can throw together a spaghetti dinner faster than we can get the pizza man to deliver. We decide whether to fix cereal or chateaubriand. We may get support and help from our male counterparts, even from our children, but most of the time, Moms are in charge of food, which means we are also in charge of nutrition. And we know more about what's good for us than ever before.

When my Mom cooked, chances were, *something* was fried—chicken, potatoes, eggs, squash, okra—and we probably had gravy to pour over it. She cooked our vegetables so long that they were sometimes hard to identify. We have made slow but reasonable progress over the last 40 years toward better and healthier eating. Some of the changes are regional. California has always led the way in trendy healthy eating. Remember all the sprout jokes? But there are some Texans who won't give up their chicken fried steak and redeye gravy without a fight or a doctor's order. On the whole, though, Americans serve fewer fried foods and more fresh fruit and vegetables than they did 30 or 40 years ago. Moms today who prepare meals at home pay much closer attention to balanced nutrition than my Mom ever did. After all, our primary concern is the health and safety of our kids, and good nutrition has become a bigger part of that. But if eating out is now a given, how much attention do we pay to the health implications of restaurant fare? Not enough, I'd say. But before getting down to cases, let's take a look at some disturbing background information.

Approximately 62 million American adults are clinically obese. Forty-one million Americans have dangerously high cholesterol levels. Thirty-seven million American adults have high blood pressure, and almost a third of them don't know it! Fifteen percent of our kids are seriously overweight, and childhood obesity is now a national concern of such epidemic proportions that the Surgeon General has gotten into the act. It is also well known that Americans consume about 20 percent more calories and 30 percent more fat in restaurants than when they eat at home.[2] Moreover, 80 percent of women are dissatisfied with their figures. Americans spend over $40 billion a year on the diet industry, and, at any given time, 25 percent of men and 45 percent of women are on a diet.[3] In the face of all these trends, health awareness is on the rise. Concerns about fat levels and other unhealthful aspects of fast food, in particular, have produced a spate of lawsuits and government investigations and a truly frightening documentary film by Morgan Spurlock called *Super Size Me.*[4] You know that fat is truly a hot topic if it gets the cover of *National Geographic Magazine* (August 2004).

How should restaurants respond to these developments? They need to recognize that their cooking styles and choice of ingredients *do* contribute to the general health of their guests, and it's time to make some changes if they want to keep them coming back.

Some restaurants are already headed in the right direction. Look at feisty Subway. It started printing the fat-and-calorie content of competing fast-food chains on its paper placemats several years ago. It was a not-so-subtle way of pointing out that by choosing one of Subway's tasty sandwiches as an alternative to the fast-food hamburger, you had done something good for yourself. Then Subway discovered Jared, who had lost 235 pounds while eating Subway sandwiches regularly! Jared now has a fan club called Friends of Jared, and all the members are reputedly losing weight with Subway sandwiches as part of their diet. Jared and his friends are in Subway commercials, on the company Web site, and in almost all other advertisements. The company seized the chance to capitalize on Jared's truly amazing success and advance the notion of healthier eating out in the process.

Now, I'm not advocating the end of hamburgers and French fries. I'm not un-American! I love them as much as any one. But as a Mom, I do love having choices that make me feel good while still fulfilling my need for speed. Locally, we have a hamburger hut called Wolfe Burgers. The hamburgers there are absolutely wonderful, but even better are the turkey burgers. So most of the time, if my family craves a good burger, we head for Wolfe Burgers. Even my son, a confirmed cheeseburger guy, can occasionally be talked into the healthier turkey burger. Of course, we still have to deal with their delicious fries and onion rings—but even they are fried in oils with low saturated fat.

I have to mention, though, that French fries are not the bane just of my existence. Americans eat an average of 28 *pounds* of French fries a year.[5] That's alarming enough, but when you consider that over 40 percent of the calories in French fries come from fat, it gets downright scary.

Perhaps the most surprising convert to the idea of fast, friendly, healthier food, at least for adults, is McDonald's. Maybe it was the threat of lawsuits that gave the company pause, or maybe the aforementioned film gave it a push, but McDonald's has done several things that give me hope. It has promised to reformulate its French fry recipe to use less fat, and it has introduced a veggie burger, a line of salads with Paul Newman's "Newman's Own" dressing, and a healthy Happy Meal for adults, with salad and bottled water. Surely, increased consumer awareness of the ever-growing evidence about the relationship between fat foods and rampant obesity helped motivate the changes. When I started research on this subject in 2000, the last thing anyone expected from most fast-food chains was a move toward healthy food choices.

Burger King kicked off its campaign to satisfy adult customers' demand for healthy choices with its low-carb burger. If McDonald's and Burger King are moving in the direction of healthy, then it's a no-brainer that others will follow. Wendy's, Hardee's, Carl's Jr., and Baja Fresh are just a few of the others who have begun to see the "lite."

And, although I don't have hard facts to back this up, I believe that McDonald's (and its competitors) finally realized that Moms were driving through, getting

Cheerful Chow for the kids, and going someplace else to get food for themselves. Even Mickey D's ads regarding these changes poked fun at themselves and singled out mothers as targets for the new salads. Smart! It's as if they are saying, "Okay, I hear you!" And trust me, if McDonald's can listen and change and still make large profits in this fickle marketplace, so can others. Since McDonald's made such a big deal about having salads, I've noticed a new line of them at Jack in the Box, Wendy's, and just about every other fast-food restaurant.

Sit-down restaurants also are moving in the right direction. Denny's, for example, has gotten into the low-fat act, too. A 2001 menu boasted a large insert on the Boca Burger, a vegetarian delight. Denny's is also one of many restaurants that have paid to be included in the Weight Watchers *Dining Out Companion,* a guide to popular chain restaurants that points out low-fat/low-calorie alternatives you might otherwise miss on the menu. I was surprised by the number of choices available even at eateries such as Taco Bell and KFC. Ruby's, a West Coast diner chain, has made eating French fries healthier. They started serving Lite Fries years ago. (If only I could get their recipe over to the folks at Wolfe Burgers!) Other major chains that have announced healthier eating initiatives include Applebee's (in partnership with Weight Watchers), Chili's, El Pollo Loco, P.F. Chang, Rubio's, Ruth's Chris Steak House, and T.G.I. Friday's.[6]

These important changes in the restaurant industry have occurred very quickly. Only four years ago, the attitude was completely different. Low-fat offerings had not been well received and came and went faster than paper dresses and belly button lights. Many Americans, burned by bad-tasting experiences, assumed that anything labeled "low" was just low in taste. (It was a variant of "anything good for me must taste bad," an attitude of children and adults whose exposure to good food is limited.) So instead of calling attention loudly to their "lite" choices, in those days many restaurants just incorporated them into the regular menu as "heart healthy" (marked by an American Heart Association heart icon). But now, restaurateurs of all types have realized at last that there is some profit in offering adults low-fat/low-carb fare. The idea of more healthy choices for adults is picking up speed and my instincts tell me that the buying power of Moms is a strong motivator for the changes. But what about our kids? What have we done for them?

Fries Are Not a Vegetable!

As a Mom, I believe that parents and restaurants have to share the responsibility for getting healthy food into our kids, and neither group gets a gold star yet. We adults finally realize, on some level, that we need to watch what we eat. We may choose *not* to, but most of us can talk the talk even if we can't walk the walk. And yet, we, who control most of what our kids eat, are raising the fattest generation of kids ever! Fat kids make for fat adults with a much higher incidence of diabetes, heart disease, and other serious health problems. In fact, a Rand Corp. study shows that obesity will cost taxpayers more than cigarettes or alcohol over the long run.[7] As caretakers, we have abdicated our responsibilities and should be ashamed. If you ask any Mom any-where how important the health of her child is, you know what the answer will be. And yet, we have deluded ourselves into thinking, for the sake of convenience, that hamburgers and fries two or three times a week are okay for our kids because, after all, they're kids.

Most middle-schoolers have to learn about the U.S. Department of Agriculture's food-guide pyramid by the seventh grade. I wonder how many people in the business of selling fries and onion rings to those kids have ever even read the back of a bread package or cereal box! Take a look at the children's menus at any of your favorite restaurants—even the ones that are pushing their low-carb options— and check them against the pyramid. At the top of the pyramid, sweets, fats, and oils are to be used only "sparingly." How often could you apply that description to kid's menu items in restaurants you patronize? Look at the vegetable and fruit categories. If your family ate all three meals at your favorite fast-food restaurant one day, could you even *find* three to five servings of vegetables or two to five servings of fruit on the menu? Morgan Spurlock couldn't balance his diet at McDonald's, much less his family's. If you eat out as often as most families do, you have to work pretty hard to find that balance because most restaurants still tend to load up kids with excessive protein, complex carbs, fat, and sugar.

The largest fast-food franchises across America know that, overall, the fat and calorie content of the food kids come to their restaurants to eat is *still* too high, despite the addition of salads and water. However, McDonald's has begun to turn at least one ship, with its lower-fat fries (assuming it implements this promise), "apple dippers" instead of fries in Happy Meals, and even an exercise video starring Ronald McDonald. If history is any clue, Burger King and the others will follow suit. (A mother can hope.)

Carrow's, a casual sit-down dining chain, has already made substantial progress just in the last two years. In 2002, its children's menu didn't pass the food pyramid test. For breakfast, they offered four choices. Three of the four contained bacon or sausage and two of the four contain other fried foods such as potatoes or French toast. The lunch and dinner choices all included French fries, except the pizza and macaroni-and-cheese options. Then, to give Carrow's credit, it allowed you to substitute mashed potatoes, fruit, or salad for fries. My thoughts at the time were that small changes in the menu could make a big difference here: *The meal comes with fruit unless you want to substitute fries for the fruit.* Offer a stuffed baked potato (reduced-calorie margarine and low-fat sour cream on the side), or a small piece of grilled chicken or fish with mashed potatoes as an entree alternative. How about a child's-size turkey burger or veggie burger?

Today's children's menu at Carrow's is a vast improvement. Three of the breakfast choices come with fruit—automatically. One of those choices is oatmeal! And while Carrow's still offers bacon and sausage, there are no fried potatoes to be seen. Lunch and dinner items come with a side of your choice, and the entrees now include grilled chicken and a turkey sandwich along with the burger, pizza, and fried chicken tenders. Can you hear the cheers coming from the Moms? I can. They'll return to Carrow's again and again.

So change is happening, in fits and starts. But there are lots of ways that fast-food restaurants, diners, and even fine dining establishments can do more to improve the well-being of kids and their families, and reap the rewards in loyal customers. Longer-lived customers are a no-brainer. A nation of healthy children is sound business policy, no matter how you look at it.

Helping Mom and the Bottom Line

My favorite idea for small children comes out of the child development books I read when my son was a baby: Serve toddlers a variety of finger foods in a muffin tin! The six little cups could be filled with ingredients that are already in the restaurant's kitchen: pieces of chicken, pieces of fruit, croutons, pieces of cheese, carrots, and celery slices—the list is endless. The muffin tins can be put on the table early in the meal—staving off grumpy fits—because preparation time is minimal. It allows the children to eat from all the major food groups, and it's healthy. If the restaurant has a salad bar, implementation of this idea is even easier. Just offer Mom a six-cup muffin tin and let her fill it herself.

Another way to improve the calorie and fat intake of adults and children is to make the healthy choices for them. Yes, it's often possible to do that without sacrificing flavor and texture. And yes, it may seem a bit paternalistic, but we are looking at an epidemic of fat in this country. Americans have fought and conquered epidemics of tooth decay, polio, tuberculosis, smallpox, and measles by working together to do the right thing. Restaurants can help do the same with the fat epidemic.

Use low-fat cheese in that grilled cheese sandwich. Use half yogurt and half mayonnaise in that ranch dressing. Use lighter oils with less saturated fat when it is appropriate. Don't be afraid of vegetables. Be creative. Personally, I would advocate fewer cooked carrots and more green beans and broccoli, but that's probably just me and cooked carrots. Of course, carrots do add color, are relatively cheap, and have a long shelf life. But maybe the simplest way to help is to use good sense when it comes to portion control for both adults and kids. I absolutely love the food at the Cheesecake Factory, but I don't like going there because the portions are so outrageously large that I feel guilty about my inability to eat it all. I don't always want to take something home, and guilty customers are not happy ones. The size of the salads is especially impractical. Maybe I could take home an uneaten half sandwich, but a day-old Cobb salad loses a lot in the translation. At least offer me a smaller portion for a reduced price. (Evidently, not many people agree with me on this issue, because Cheesecake Factory is, hands down, one of the most successful restaurant chains in the nation.) Do the same thing for children: Offer half-portions of items on the adult menu at a reduced price. Some restaurants will serve half-orders on request, but in a family restaurant, it should be noted clearly in the menu.

If restaurateurs presented the healthier alternatives with the same care as they do the less healthy ones—instead of using an asterisk and fine print to inform parents and children of choices—then "what everyone wants" just might change. The National Restaurant Association, which represents all types of restaurateurs across the country, might accuse me of trying to pin our national obesity problems on the food service industry. I'm not. I'm trying to pin some of the solutions on it. Five years ago, it would not have been receptive. An article in *Restaurant Hospitality* in 2000 suggested the following as the best response to the "fat police":

> *You, as a food service operator, represent the restaurant industry.*
> *And it is an industry of choice. You give your customers the right*
> *to choose what they want to eat and how much of it they want*
> *to eat. You are not forcing them to walk through your front door*
> *and eat there. They make the choice to eat there in the first*
> *place. Keep in mind that your job as a restaurant operator is to*
> *keep your customers happy, not to monitor what they eat. The*
> *restaurant industry gives its customers a lot of choices, even the*
> *choice not to clean their plates.[8]*

Cut to 2004. Now the association offers a downloadable guide to healthy eating and advice to restaurants that want to offer healthy alternatives. This change in attitude is the direct result of the demands made by Moms and other customers for healthier fare. We had to yell pretty loud before the changes became widespread, and I know that a large part of the response was due to dollar signs rather than to any sense of altruism. The unbelievable popularity of the Atkins diet, the South Beach diet, old standbys like Weight Watchers and Jenny Craig, and innumerable other programs, to the tune of $40 billion a year,[9] helped make it clear there was money to be made. That's fine. A Mom will take what she can get.

If you are one of the over 875,000 restaurant operators in the country and you are moving in this direction, I applaud you—regardless of your motivation! The rest of you, keep in mind that even though you can't force customers in your door, you can spend lots of money trying to entice them in. And once you get them, it is good for your business to keep them. So if it really is about choice, then broaden the choices. If it really is about what's best for your customer, then include lots of healthy things in those choices. Admit that consumers are getting smarter and pickier. Get ready to ride the wave now because, as a Mom, I appreciate the help and I will reward that help with my money. But if you don't want to help, then as a customer, I can always take my business elsewhere. It's not wise to underestimate the power of the Mom Factor.

Family Friendly Is More Than Food: The Welcome Mat

In the aftermath of 9/11, family togetherness seems even more important than it did before. Many Moms want to cocoon more often with their husbands and kids, even when they go out to eat. So they want to head for a family-friendly environment. Good (and, we hope, healthful) food is primary, but how does a mother know that a place is family-friendly? For one thing, mothers talk to other mothers. Forty-seven percent of women will recommend a restaurant to a friend.[10] Mothers have their own built-in rating system, and we might give a so-so place a second chance, but rarely a third. If families are part of a restaurant's core business, their importance needs to shine in all aspects of the dining experience so the word will get out.

Families ought to be pretty hard for most restaurants to ignore. Over 56 percent of all money spent on food away from home came from households with children.[11] There are over 32 million such family households that have a Mom in charge. Approximately 71 percent of those mothers work.[12] Even if we *don't* assume that working mothers are somewhat more likely to eat out than their stay-at-home sisters, that's an extraordinarily large pool of potential customers for family restaurants. And it doesn't even include all those Grandmoms out there, who also take the kids out to eat. This is not brain surgery. Restaurants that want to raise their revenues can do so by putting up a sign: "Family-Friendly" or "Children Welcome." And then, of course, they have to show they mean it. Identifying a place as kid-friendly is extremely important. In my own survey, Moms listed two main reasons for going to a certain restaurant for a sit-down dinner: good food and kid-friendliness.

Starbucks is one place where that sign is up, even though it's not actually hanging in the window. No one would confuse this coffeehouse with the Rainbow Room, and I realize that you are either a Starbucks aficionado or you hate the place. Still, from the beginning, it has been very family-friendly. On any given morning, in neighborhoods all over America, you can walk into Starbucks and find Moms and babies enjoying a little break. Starbucks offers high chairs, kids' drinks, and a great attitude. Mom gets her latte and a few precious minutes in grown-up land listening to music that doesn't put her to sleep, and smelling something other than whirled peas. And baby-less folks get to smile and coo at the little ones. Or not.

Even though it's not a typical restaurant, Starbucks works for me as a family *establishment*. So what is it, exactly, that makes a good family *restaurant*? To me, it's a place where children are welcomed, not just accommodated. That's an attitude that starts with the manager and host or hostess. Most mothers are really good at reading body language. They have to be. They spend the first 18 to 36 months of a child's life interpreting wants and needs with few language clues. So when the person at the podium looks at your child as if you have a warthog on a leash, then you know you are not in a family-friendly restaurant. But if that person smiles and greets both you and your kids with evident pleasure, then you're more likely than not to return—assuming the rest of the experience follows suit.

A mother I know won't take her children into a new restaurant if it doesn't offer a children's menu. To her, the children's menu is the signal that the restaurant really wants her family business. If the menu or the placemat offers the kids something to color or puzzles to do, so much the better. It is true that children, especially the smaller ones, are not good at sitting and waiting, but most love to doodle and draw. Another way to occupy them is to put butcher paper on the table along with a bucket of crayons. The many restaurants that do this have found that adults often enjoy doodling as much as the children. Denny's goes a step further, offering three-dimensional fun: they provide a small bucket of interconnecting pieces to play with while awaiting the meal—and they will also sell you a box of them on your way out.

I have to say that I'm of two minds about playing at the table. At home, I did not allow my son to bring toys to the table, and I daresay you don't allow it either. The toys and colors have become bribes to ensure that no one acts up or demands too much of our attention—especially in public. The price we pay is that children now expect to be entertained while eating, no matter where they are.

I know I sound like a cross old lady when I say it, but too often in America we have gotten away from the idea that mealtime is the time for interacting and sharing with the whole family. If nothing else, it is an opportunity to teach good manners and listening skills—another completely old-fashioned idea. On top of my strong personal opinions on this subject comes new research indicating that isolated eating—whether at home in front of the tube, in school or at the local hamburger joint—contributes to obesity. Not only is what we eat of importance, but how and where we eat, too. We tend to eat healthier when we treat mealtime as an opportunity to bring the family together. It's something to think about.

Several other clues tell Moms that a restaurant really wants children. If families are truly welcome, then the table and wall decorations should be appropriate. A South Pasadena, California, restaurant called Wild Thyme has a carousel horse suspended from the ceiling, a real pint-sized crowd pleaser. In contrast, my family had to stop going to one local Mexican restaurant because of its mural of a bullfight, complete with the *faena*, or killing of the bull. The art had my very young animal lover almost in tears.

There should be no top-heavy vases full of pretty flowers that little hands can't resist. No expensive sculpture on the back of the booth that just invites greasy fingers. Nothing that prompts the proprietor or personnel to say or think, "Please don't touch."

Seating is important, too. Booths make it easier to assist little ones, and there's a lot more freedom of movement. If only tables are available, high chairs or clip-on chairs for the toddlers are a must. High chairs at self-serve restaurants need to have wheels on the back so that a Mom, with a baby in her arms, can get the thing to the table. That kind of thought about the reality of eating out with children goes a long way. There ought to be comfortable chairs of the proper height for the older children, as well. You should try eating a meal at a table that's chest-high!

A good seating arrangement extends beyond the types of chairs available. It's only sensible and obvious to seat families with young children away from the bar area. Adults in bars rarely want to be serenaded by crying babies or laughing children. On the other hand, here's an idea whose time has come—the family sports "bar." ESPN Zone may be the ultimate sports dining experience, but you have to be 21 to enter the Screening Room, where the big game of the day is shown, after 5:00 p.m. Why couldn't there be a family version of this room, where Mom, Dad, and the kids could eat and watch the Yankees battle the Red Sox or the Pistons sink the Lakers?

Child-friendly restaurants need to have a reasonable noise level. A hushed environment suitable for a London men's club is totally intimidating to parents and children. In that situation, bribes are an essential part of Mom's behavior management arsenal. My friend Jody says that her ancient aunt has a rule, "I can only be adorable for three hours." Well, most children have a much shorter adorable span. Good music and an upbeat—but not frenetic—atmosphere can extend that span.

More and more Moms (and dads) are aware of the dangers of secondhand smoke, so it is vital that the restaurants that still have smoking sections make sure that they also have proper ventilation. I won't take my son to a restaurant if we have to sit anywhere near the smoking section, unless the fans work really well.

Mothers universally look for cleanliness in a restaurant, be it sit-down or fast-food. The topic came up over and over again in my survey. If the place isn't clean, the chances of a return visit are almost nonexistent. Mothers notice things because they are forever taking babies' hands out of stuff. They are quick to spot grimy countertops, dirty floors, bathrooms that have been mopped in a circle (you know the type: all the corners are black with gunk), and trash spilling out of the containers. It's a real turnoff. One of the mothers in my survey labeled her local national-al fast-food eatery, "Horrible service. Dirty. Disgusting food." You *really* don't want Moms to label your restaurant like that. And Moms do talk!

Last, but certainly not least, are the wait staff. I ranted about retail customer service in Chapter 1 and Chapter 2, and much of what I said there applies to restaurants, too. It's true that under certain circumstances, customers (and that includes you) are willing to sacrifice attentive service for other considerations such as speed, convenience—and did I mention speed? Fast-food places with limited (extremely limited lately, I might say) service do have their place. But poor customer service in a sit-down restaurant makes even less sense than at Penney's. The waitperson is simply pulling money out of his or her own pocket by treating customers poorly. Proper training and high management expectations are essential. Just as in any business, if the personnel respond positively to me and to my family, then I am much more likely to turn into a loyal customer. We have been eating at one local restaurant,

Kathleen's, for more than 15 years. I went there when I was pregnant, when my son was in a baby carrier, after his first Little League All-Star game, with Granddad and Grandma, and for Mother's Day Brunch. Why such loyalty? Because after about the fourth or fifth visit, the owner called us by name and the waitresses remembered us. They got to know us so well they would ask about anybody who was missing from the party. *How's your son? Where are your mom and dad tonight?* They didn't roll their eyes in horror when my son spilled something on the floor, or blanch when he ordered the shrimp and pasta with tomato sauce instead of the garlic cream sauce. Often, schedules were so tight that my son had to do his homework while we were eating. That was fine. They would ask him how school was going. If we ever had a problem with the food or a special request, they took care of it without question. It was clear that our business was important to them and that they liked us—all of us. So we go back—again and again.

In restaurants, as in retail, management sets the tone. In my survey, I found that IHOP (International House of Pancakes) got both raves and rants. But the IHOP that got the raves was in the Midwest. The IHOP that got the rants was in California. Obviously, customer service mattered more to one management team than it did to another. It doesn't matter whether the restaurant is individually owned and operated or part of a huge national chain, success depends not so much on rules but on common courtesy and good sense.

I'm not alone in this demand for service. In my pilot survey, 88 percent of the people who responded to the question concerning improvement in sit-down restaurants or fast-food restaurants said that there was a need for better service. One mother said, "I would like to be treated more like a valued customer than a number. I want to be appreciated." Mothers wanted their orders filled correctly, and if mistakes were made, they wanted them corrected without hassle or attitude or finger-pointing. You'll find the same customer-service chorus girls dancing in each chapter of this book: *Treat me as though I matter to you, and I will come back and spend my money.* Kick, sidestep, kick!

Listen to Your Mother

Eating out has become a necessity in most families because of the time constraints in modern living. Now, more than ever, there is a need for places where a family can sit down to dinner together and enjoy the time and the food. I know that as a mother, it's really very simple—I will pay for that opportunity.

Endnotes

1. National Restaurant Association, www.restaurant.org; National Restaurant Association news release, July 20, 2000.

2. American Heart Association, "Overweight and Obesity Statistics" (www.americanheart.org/downloadable/heart/1077869615722FS15OVR4.pdf); and *Heart Disease and Stroke Statistics—2004 Update* (Dallas, Texas: American Heart Association, 2003), pp. 17, 28; *Newsweek*, September 22, 2003, p. 60; *Food Service Director*, December 15, 2001, p.60.

3. National Eating Disorders Association, "Eating Disorders and Their Precursors," www.nationaleatingdisorders.org, 2002.

4. Directed by Morgan Spurlock, www.supersizeme.com.

5. *Los Angeles Times*, July 12, 2002, page C1.

6. For an updated list, go to www.restaurant.org.

7. Rand Corporation, "The Effects of Obesity, Smoking and Drinking on Medical Problems and Costs," *Health Affairs*, vol. 21, no. 2, March/April 2002.

8. Sheila R. Cohn and Steven F. Grover, "Doing Battle with the 'Fat' Police," *Restaurant Hospitality*, December 2000, p. 64.

9. National Eating Disorders Association, "Know Dieting: Risks and Reasons to Stop," www.nationaleatingdisorders.org, 2002.

10. Linda P. Morton, "Segmenting Publics by Gender," *Public Relations Quarterly*, Winter 1999, vol. 44, issue 4, p. 41, sixth in a series of articles on market segmentation.

11. Karen Gardner, "The Boomer Echo," *Restaurants USA*, March 1997, citing a National Restaurant Association analysis of U.S. Bureau of Labor Statistics data pertaining to 1994. This article is archived at www.restaurant.org/rusa/magArticle.cfm?ArticleID=509.

12. U.S. Bureau of the Census, American FactFinder Web site (factfinder.census.gov), Detailed Tables, Table P18: Household Size, Household Type, and Presence of Own Children; U.S. Bureau of Labor Statistics, USDL04-719, "Employment Characteristics of Families in 2003," April 20, 2004, news release.

Chapter 4

Real Family Entertainment Makes Memories

everal years ago, I met my friend Andrea for lunch at a local Thai restaurant. Over our *mee krob*, we talked about families, and children, and events in our lives. She mentioned that she had recently taken her children to three different birthday parties at a new location-based entertainment center run by one of the largest entertainment companies in the world. The experiences had not amused her. "There was no place for parents to sit comfortably and watch the children play. The sightlines were horrible. It was very easy for children to get lost behind things. It was an uncomfortable place. I could see what they were trying to do, but I swear, this place was designed by well-meaning bald-headed men who never had to run after small children!" It was Andrea's way of saying that the place wasn't family-friendly and that no one involved in its design had thought it through from the parent's perspective. I'm not saying that this lack of attention to family was necessarily what doomed the concept, but the company dropped the whole idea of location-based family entertainment centers within months of our lunch.

If I mention the words "family entertainment" to other mothers, the reaction is often some variation of "It hasn't been done yet." Family entertainment, from my point of view *within* the entertainment industry, has always seemed problematic. How can you design and build for something that is so hard to define? Today, we recognize that there are two-parent families, single-parent families, same-sex-partner families, grandparent families, combined families, and families of unrelated individuals. There are families with babies, small children, teenagers, and every possible combination of age groups. The only constant—the only factor that *must* be present—is an understanding among those in the group that this social unit is "our family."

For a real insight into the difficulty of confining family to one definition, look at Disney's 2002 animated feature *Lilo and Stitch*. Stitch is a six-armed, furry, blue alien created in a test tube, looking for a place to belong. He winds up in a "family" made up of two other aliens, a pair of sisters, a surfer dude, and a social worker. Only the sisters are blood relatives, but the movie makes clear by the end that this group is Stitch's new family. How do you define entertainment for a group that diverse? And, more specifically, how do you create a place where mothers—the decision makers on the majority of family entertainment outings—are, at the very least, comfortable?

It's a question that the family entertainment industry has been chewing on for years, and I don't think they've arrived at a definitive answer yet. There is a convention in Las Vegas every year called Fun Expo. It's one of a handful of trade shows for those involved in family entertainment. The majority of attendees are those who run arcades and miniature golf, laser tag, and go-cart facilities. These outfits operate under the heading of family entertainment centers, or FECs. On an early 1990s trip to this small but enlightening show, I attended a panel filled with the celebrities of the business, including one remarkable woman named Celia Pearce. In a speech on the future of family entertainment, she looked us all in the eye and said, "What family decides to go out and shoot each other on Saturday night?"

She was referring to the typical video games available in arcades around the country. Even though she gave her speech many years ago and the furor over violent games has died down a bit, arcades are still not designed for families. And yet these arcades—full of games that for the most part can be played by only one player at a time—call themselves "family entertainment centers." In fact, their main demographic appeal is to 14 to 25-year-old males. Pearce's point at the time was that the games offered in these arcades have nothing to do with family. However, the money spent in them most certainly does because it comes from Mom's purse!

Family Entertainment Centers

I have taken my son to FECs in almost every place we traveled—from the small town of L'Aquila, Italy, where he discovered an interactive soccer game that allowed the player to kick a real soccer ball mounted on the base of the game, to Lone Pine, California, where there were snowboarding games installed next to the ice cream parlor. He's driven Go-Karts in Ventura and played Skee Ball in Las Vegas and flown a virtual hang glider in New Orleans. He's had birthday parties at the SpeedZone and taken friends and family to play miniature golf. That, by the way, was the only truly family activity at any FEC we've ever been to. For the most part, my role—and the role of every other mother at FECs—is that of cash cow and cheerleader.

That doesn't mean I won't continue to patronize FECs. I will. I even like going to some of them. One of my favorites is SpeedZone in City of Industry, California. It really is intended for teenagers and adults. They make that quite clear in their advertising and on their Web site, although they don't exclude younger kids. They offer a set of three racetracks, with three different kinds of cars, and a miniature golf course. There's also a nice, clean, well-lighted arcade, with an emphasis on sports and skill-based games, and an elevated bar and restaurant. I can sit down, have a decent lunch and a cold beer, and still keep the kids in sight in the arcade. I know a lot of parents would object to the sale of alcohol, but we usually take our young groups early in the day, knowing full well that the crowd's age drifts upward the later it gets. The employees are courteous, hardworking, and hip. I don't race, but I could if I weren't a chicken. Many adults do race with their teenagers and, of course, the kids love it when they can beat Dad. Half a day there costs me about $40 to $50 per kid, including lunch.

FECs can get good marks from me—even if they don't have activities for the whole family—if they convey a message Moms like. My research uncovered a very special FEC that certainly gets this Mom's seal of approval for good role-modeling. Fun Spot Action Park in Orlando, Florida, is on a mission.[1] It invites teenagers to drive its courses as if they were drunk! As part of a community outreach program, this Go-Kart track works with the Florida Highway Patrol so that teenagers get a reality check regarding the hazards of driving drunk. Using special goggles that emulate the vision of someone who has just had four beers in one hour, the kids have to drive the track and avoid signs and other obstacles before the officer pulls them over to show them what a DUI arrest is like. It's especially appealing to the 14- to 18-year-old crowd. All of them are cocksure they can ace the course, but they sing a different tune when they see the videotape of their exploits. Not only does Fun Spot sponsor this terrific program, it does so for free. The plus for the company is direct involvement in the community and, because only eight kids can race at a time, a captive audience for the arcade. I would definitely spend money there in support of its community outreach.

Another family attraction displaying similar evidence of a social conscience is Funtasticks Family Fun Park in Tucson, Arizona. A local bank, the local ad federation, and the local humane society have honored it over the years for excellence in community service. Funtasticks has created a Community Support Calendar that combines involvement with great public relations. Each month a different non-profit agency can schedule a fundraiser or set up a display or information table, or the park will donate a gift to the agency. In addition to the monthly program, Funtasticks does special events and parties for selected groups. The community involvement also helps workplace morale—in 2002, Funtasticks won a regional award for best place to work!

At one of the most recent Fun Expo Conventions, the buzz over the Next Big Thing really got me thinking about Pearce's pointed question and Mom's place in all this. According to owners around the country, FECs are betting on larger profits with paintball, skate parks, and extreme sports. Mom, don't you just long for the opportunity to splatter your daughter and your husband in a game of paintball on Saturday night? And don't you wanna grab your skateboard or jump on a BMX bike and eat a little dirt? Sorry, this is not family entertainment. Why even try to fool us? This is teenage boy entertainment. The teenage girls come mostly because that's where they can find the boys.

Retailers have learned that women generally prefer to spend money at places that have some sort of social or community conscience. Not only that, but as Moms, we are striving to teach our children the same values. Gen Xers prefer to spend their money where it matters. Both Fun Spot and Funtasticks certainly have a better understanding of human values than the paintball set. And, speaking as a Mom, that is worth a lot. So I would spend money at either place without rancor, even if I weren't having the time of my life.

Amusement Parks

Attractions other than FECs also consider themselves family entertainment. Millions of families each year go to regional amusement parks, fairs, and traveling carnivals, whose rides and refreshments are very similar to those of FECs.

The International Association of Amusement Parks and Attractions[2] reported that, in 2003, some 322 million people visited the 600 theme and amusement parks in America. IAAPA doesn't separate theme parks from amusement parks, and you might wonder why I put them in different categories and different chapters for purposes of the Mom Factor. I see theme parks as destination attractions with a huge tourist base, able to support a two- or three-day stay. Amusement parks, on the other hand, are definitely day trips, and rely on local attendance more than tourists. In addition, amusement parks are known mainly for their roller coasters and thrill rides. While many have theming and license recognizable characters, they usually do not attempt to create an immersive environment. It's all about higher, faster, and scarier. They dot the regional landscapes of America from coast to coast. Amusement parks can range in size from the 15-acre Wonderland Park[3] in Amarillo, Texas— which my son swears is better than Disneyland, in part, because they have Dippin' Dots Ice Cream—to the Six Flags chain, which owns 30 parks worldwide (including some water parks).

Most amusement parks are not really intended to amuse adults, and certainly not Moms and grandmoms. They are intended to be thrilling, wonderful places for children and teens. They are also places to challenge parental authority. "Mom, I dare you to ride the Super-Duper Loopity Loop with me!" Now, there are Moms who will actually accept this dare, and I admire them more than I can say. They are fearless and know better than to eat chilidogs and cotton candy beforehand. I am not currently one of them (although I've done my share of loopity loops). And since fathers are often kids in man suits who love dares and thrive on competition, you'll see lots of them barreling through the air on wooden roller coasters, momentarily without a care in the world! Among the many Moms I have talked to about thrill rides, the usual comment is, "I would never get on one of those things. I send them out with their dad."

There are times, however, when Mom must go, and some times when she wants to go. If you operate a park and want her to enjoy herself and be willing to bring the kids back, then consult the checklist below, which is based on elements of the Mom Factor. Remember, there's very little entertainment for me other than watching my children have fun. So if you want me to spend money, then I need a few things. These are basic to any place that I might take my family, and the absence of one or more will definitely affect my length of stay and my return visits.

■ **Seating.** Seating in the shade is mandatory. I need places to sit where I can comfortably watch my kids. They like to show off for me, and I like to cheer them on. Make it easy. This seems like a no-brainer, but it's amazing how often seating is an afterthought. Even *theme* parks too often seem to forget comfort between rides. (Several years ago one of the biggest theme park companies around had spent many millions of dollars on a new park and had not provided enough seating. They soon realized their mistake—thanks in part, no doubt, to irate Moms who spoke their minds—and spent a lot of money correcting that deficiency. Now, there is a bench every five feet! But what took so long?) Water parks are the worst. The assumption seems to be that if you are there, you are in the water. Do you know how few Moms do bathing suits in public? Too bad if you just want to sit and watch your child slide down the slides. There aren't nearly enough observation areas in most parks, although Hurricane Harbor in Valencia, California, a Six Flags water park, does a pretty good job. It actually has small grandstands at the end of some of the slides so that parents can comfortably watch the show.

■ **Safety and Service.** I also need to feel that my kids are safe running around the park. Gated entrances and nice, friendly, obvious security people help. Employees need to make me feel wanted, not as though I'm ruining their day. I know that employee training is costly and sometimes difficult, but you only get one chance to impress a Mom. If your employees are rude and inattentive, then the chances of a return visit plummet. I will drive hours out of my way, if I know that I will be treated well. (Cue the customer service chorus line: And step, kick, cross-step, kick!)

■ **Respect.** Your courtesy and customer service need to extend to my teen-agers, too. It is no longer permissible in this society to judge someone simply by his or her looks, if it ever was. You can't assume that tattoos, piercings, purple hair, chains, and spikes mean anything about the kid they adorn. If you own and operate a place that will attract teens—like an amusement park full of death-defying roller coasters—then you have to accept your clientele just the way they come. Whatever security rules you have must be clearly posted and uniformly applied. Any policies you have must be applied consistently to every race, creed, color, and costume. You can't have your security guards hassling the kids with metal spikes on their hats. You can't have guards hassling girls with bare midriffs and belly button rings. And you can't have them stereotyping guys wearing saggies—unless you have a posted park policy against these things. These are my children. I respect their rights to individuality and so must you. If I get even a hint that you have singled out my son or daughter or their friends for no reason other than their nose rings, then I, my kids, and my money are history. Please remember, when you factor in the Mother's circle of influence, it's not just my business you will lose. I'll spread the word to everyone I know. I understand that since 9/11, security everywhere is tougher and more exclusionary. It's an unpleasant fact of life. We all have made and will continue to make compromises. But common sense must prevail. Liberty spikes, tattoos, and leather pants don't denote a terrorist, any more than crew cuts, a dark suit, and dark glasses denote a Secret Service agent. If teens are part of your target audience, then treat them respectfully. As a Mom, not only will I appreciate it, I'll reward you.

■ **Cleanliness.** I need the place to be clean. Not necessarily "sparkling white." But somebody needs to be on constant trash duty and keep the aisles and waiting areas tolerable.

■ **Clocks.** I need lots of clocks so that I can tell my kids—who don't often remember their watches—that they need to meet me at a certain time, and I need to know they will have no excuses.

■ **Value.** I need to feel as though I'm getting value for the money I spend. I don't expect bargains, but overinflated food and drink prices will indeed keep me from coming back. Parking that costs more than half the price of a ticket is a turnoff, especially since I will be walking miles to the entrance anyway. Reasonably priced stroller rentals and lockers also keep me from feeling victimized.

■ **Food.** Menu choices that include something other than "fried everything" make an impression. You might even be bold and daring and open real sit-down restaurants serving good food.

■ **Bathrooms.** The basic things are sometimes the most important. I am reminded of another convention in Las Vegas when another very smart woman was speaking to yet another audience of people trying to understand family entertainment. Kathy McHugh, then president of Knutson-McHugh Consulting, said, "If you want to design family entertainment, start with the bathrooms." Believe me, she knows what she's talking about. Clean, safe, clean, easy-to-navigate-with-a-stroller, clean bathrooms are near the top of most Moms' checklists for any place they have to go with small children. When given the opportunity to suggest a needed change at family entertainment venues, 20 percent of Moms in my survey wanted larger, cleaner bathrooms.

■ **Entertainment.** You definitely need to consider entertaining me. Stage shows, music, exhibits, demonstrations, massages, landscaping, cyber cafés, nonsouvenir shopping—any or all of these will encourage the non–roller coaster Mom to stay and spend money.

So if you want my children and my pocketbook to be allowed to return, pay attention to these elements of design and execution. They make an impression on Moms.

Other Family Attractions

I have always been a fan of the circus, even in this day and time when it isn't so politically correct. It was a big event in the middlin' size Texas town in which I grew up. It came every year, just like the wheat harvest, and it was thrilling. One year (I think I was 16), I actually had the nerve to knock on the door of the circus office and ask how to join. My heart's desire was to be a bally girl, dress in a sparkling costume and ride an elephant. I know I gave my own Mom a heart attack! I didn't go, but I came awfully close. For me, the circus has always been able to transport me to another time and place. The smells of popcorn and hay, the brilliant colors, the calliope music, the exotic animals, even the silly made-in-China souvenirs were wonderful. It seemed a microcosm of the world, with people and animals from everywhere. Where else could a small-town girl like me have that kind of international experience? The memories of that magic made it inevitable that I would want to share it with my husband and my son. Sharing memories is at the very heart of the best family entertainment.

In all the design meetings I've attended, the kids drive the entertainment design. It's the kid's side of the equation that defines the fun—roller coasters, dark rides, shooting galleries, water slides, skate parks, and so on. Clearly, that is a formula that has worked for places like Six Flags, Busch Gardens, Paramount Parks, and others. But there are places that really engage the whole family, attractions that cover a wide spectrum of human possibilities and experience. Often, they work because they appeal to both head and heart—Mom's and everybody else's.

One particular group has very successfully tapped into the hearts of people of all ages with a combination of art, acrobatics, humor, and mystery. Our family first saw Cirque du Soleil when it raised its tent down on the beach in Santa Monica, California, in the mid-1980s. We had no children then, but that didn't matter—we took *our* parents. Just walking into the tent transported us to another place, and the show itself was truly magical. Since then, we have seen several Cirque du Soleil shows, and they continue to offer something for almost everyone. Cirque officials do not keep demographic statistics on their audiences, but they can tell you that by 2002, 33 million people had seen the shows since that first traveling company opened in 1984. In 2002, they projected that 60,000 people would see some kind of Cirque show every weekend! Today, Cirque has four permanent homes—three in Las Vegas and one, interestingly enough, at Disney World in Orlando. I wish I could adequately describe what makes a visit to Cirque so memorable, but it is beyond description. Suffice it to say that Cirque does what all attraction designers hope to do—it appeals to all the senses without ever being predictable. You laugh, you gasp, you hold your breath in anticipation, but you are never bored. The older you are, the more the mystery of it all deepens. It is a wonderful, if expensive (tickets in Las Vegas run $75 to $100 each), place to entertain the whole family.[4]

Another kind of something-for-everyone attraction is the fair. There are about 3,200 fairs every year in towns across America: state fairs, county fairs, national fairs, agricultural fairs, mid-state fairs, and tri-state fairs.[5] Fairs are interesting creatures. In some ways, they are remnants of another time and place. Most state fairs got their starts in the mid-1800s. The idea was to create a place where farmers and manufacturers around the state could show off their products to the world. In 2003, the New York State Fair drew more than 32,000 entrants in events from pie-baking to pigeon-raising, biggest tomato to most beautiful quilt, best wine to best cow. And over a million people attended the fair during its 12-day run. The official history of the Texas State Fair notes that the fair today is much as it was in 1886, "a mix of what's new, what's best, how fast does it go, who will be there, and when does it start . . . ."[6] The midway; the rides; the incredible products such as knives that cut through concrete or vacuum cleaners that suck up airplane parts; the animal barns full of cows, sheep, horses, pigs, llamas, and alpacas—all make marvelous fun for families.

Fairs in America are a time machine, providing cross-generational shared experiences for everyone from toddlers to grandpas. Where else but a fair can eight-year-old Thomas enter his collection of Pez dispensers or padlocks or playing cards and win first prize in his age category for best collection? And where else could I *see* these amazing collections? My own memories of a Midwestern regional fair include the bunting that was draped all over town in the days before the fair opened. It meant an official day off from school so that we could get a different kind of education. It meant beautiful horses and the thrill of the carnival and the mystery of the midway. In the 1960s, you could still find a two-headed snake or a bearded lady there. Today, the midway is different (thank goodness) and the rides and games are similar to those offered at small amusement parks. But it's still possible to win your best girl a huge stuffed bear, eat your way through every variation of fried food from bread to Snickers (no noticeable move toward healthy fare here!), compare the merits of shoats and goats, and see the latest in mops and massagers, spreads and spas.

The larger fairs offer terrific entertainment: headlining stars, monster truck competitions, horse racing, midget-car races—it's hard to beat a fair for variety. In addition, there's usually one near you. It doesn't require a long trip or even an overnight stay. It can cost you as little as the price of admission or as much as the price of admission and a new eight-seat spa! And it meets other Mom Factor criteria for worthwhile experiences: it is immersive, engaging, educational, and fun for the *whole* family.

Another often overlooked attraction that offers true family fun is the factory tour. I know it sounds almost as corny as going to the circus. But consider that the Coca Cola Museum in Atlanta, Georgia, attracts more visitors than any other single destination in the city, and you might begin to understand. (Coca Cola is currently creating an entirely new experience that will replace the current version. I guarantee it will be worth a visit.)

The common denominator in factory tours is the idea of process. Kids love process and so do adults. How does that thingamajig work? How do you get flakes from an ear of corn? What do you get when you mix this stuff with that? So, in Hershey, Pennsylvania, who can resist a tour that promises mysteries solved and kisses at the end? The Hershey Chocolate Factory Tour is really a dark ride about the making of chocolate and actually takes place far from the factory. The best part is that it's free. Kellogg's Cereal City in Battle Creek, Michigan, offers a similar experience. The original factory tour has been replaced by a factory tour attraction that tells the story of how cereal is made. This attraction isn't free, but it does include samples and the chance to meet Tony the Tiger. Just outside Waterbury, Vermont, you'll find Ben and Jerry's, the makers of Vermont's Finest Ice Cream. The tour charges $3 for adults, but children under 12 are free. It includes a *moovie*, lessons in community involvement, and a chance to see the real ice-cream production line. And, of course, there are samples at the end. This is less amusement park and more traditional factory tour. So is the Visitor's Center of the Tillamook Cheese Factory in Tillamook, Oregon. This free self-guided tour showcases the entire cheese-making process—"from cow to mouth." Lots of samples, an ice cream counter, a store, and a restaurant round out the experience.

Moms are attracted to these kinds of activities for many reasons. They are different from museums on the one hand, and amusement parks on the other. There's no feeling that if you've seen one, you've seen them all because no two factory tours are the same. They offer the opportunity for everyone in the family to learn something in a painless and even entertaining way. They usually reflect local history, so there's a feeling that you have been somewhere. Even the souvenirs seem special. And don't forget the samples! These tours aren't expensive; in fact, many are free. All this contributes to a feeling of real value for time spent. Finally, these tours pay more attention to customer service than most attractions because each speaks for a brand that wants your loyalty.

We Love the Outdoors!

My friend Judy and her family have spent a lot of vacations camping and hiking and exploring. Her sons and her husband have all been involved in the Boy Scouts for many years (all three were Eagle Scouts!). She, too, loves the mountains; only now that the boys are grown, she's gotten very fond of a good bed and hot shower as opposed to a tent. One of her best stories, now family legend, concerns the five national parks, two state parks, one national monument, one Meteor Crater, one national recreation area, white water rafting, and a visit to an outlet mall, all in a six-day vacation! By the time they got to Bryce Canyon, Utah, they had stopped at so many scenic overlooks that her husband Eric said, "Just stay in the car. They all look the same." While she doesn't recommend such a trip for everyone (professional drivers only, closed track), she highly recommends staying in the national parks with kids. "For years, Eric has always remembered that trip as a terrible one (maybe because he did most of the driving). But the kids and I had a blast. We certainly created some great family memories."

FamilyFun, a magazine published by Disney, puts together an annual list of places families go for fun, based on a survey of its subscriber base. Its 2000 and 2001 Family-Friendly Travel Awards provided a good look at pre-9/11 family attractions. It divided the country into five regions and asked the locals within each region to recommend must-see family attractions. Both years, the list of the 12 highest-scoring attractions from coast to coast included national parks and monuments (about half the list) and museums and theme parks (about a quarter each), with the occasional zoo for additional zest.

Imagine that! National parks outrank all other regional attractions as the place families recommend for other families. It's easy to gauge the reasons for their popularity if you consider the Mom Factor. To begin with, national parks offer activity and information in a setting that cannot be duplicated, and the authenticity of a park experience is indisputable. A national park is immersive. Just wander down the trail a bit at the Grand Canyon, and the rest of the world disappears. Talk about an attraction that engages all the senses: red stone vistas and bracing breezes full of the scent of pine and the songs of coyotes! It's educational. You can't help but learn something at a national park, and the kids never know what hit them. National parks also represent good value. The entrance fee for a carload of folks at the most popular parks is still about $20, and once you are in, you can spend as much or as little as your budget can afford. And let's not forget, national parks also have bathroom facilities—if not particularly decorative, then at least numerous, and they're pretty clean under the circumstances, all of which is important, as we have established. Campsites in national parks are as sought after as weekend reservations at the Red Door Spa—and almost as hard to come by during the peak seasons. As a result, the National Park Service reported that, in the year 2003, some 266 million people visited one of the places within its care.[7]

If there is a common denominator among the wide variety of places on the *FamilyFun* list, perhaps it's that each of them leaves every visitor with a feeling of wonder and delight—regardless of age! My own family loves Yosemite. We always go in the winter, looking for snow and sparse crowds. We find it to be a magical place. On our last trip, we saw coyotes, a black bear, and lots of deer and squirrels. My son went skiing for the first time. He even ice-skated in the shadow of Half Dome. We took walks, and at night, we looked at the stars or played board games and put together puzzles. Our sense of leaving behind everyday cares was palpable.

When I was young, my family often vacationed in New Mexico, and we always stopped at Capulin Mountain, a national monument right off Highway 87 on the road from Dalhart to Raton. (That places it for you, doesn't it?) There's a nice visitor center on the edge of this perfect extinct volcano cone, and if you come at the right time of year, the rocks and scrub are covered with ladybugs! The park is in the middle of nowhere, but it has its own magic. So when I got married, I had to take my husband there, and then much later we had to take our son. It's only a pleasant two-hour diversion, but trust me, millions of ladybugs crawling around the top of a volcano and an endless view of deep blue sky and ancient lava-beds can be very entertaining to a three-year-old and his thirty-something parents.

Did you know that the Liberty Bell and Independence Hall are in a national park? Independence National Historical Park, to be exact, right in the middle of Philadelphia. With more than 5 million visitors annually, this park is home to many touchstones of American history. It is also home to an attraction that really rates high on the Mom Factor scale. The Lights of Liberty is a multimedia walking tour of Old Philadelphia, complete with 3D sound, that traces the beginning of the fight for freedom in the land that would become the United States of America. It features a terrific script created from actual letters and speeches written by the protagonists and read by such worthy actors as Ossie Davis, Charlton Heston, Frank Langella, and Claire Bloom; a fabulous score played by the Philadelphia Orchestra; and the dramatic lighting and direction of the Miziker Entertainment Group. It also has all the things that Moms look for in an entertainment venue.

It's immersive. Because Lights of Liberty takes place on the streets of Philadelphia after sunset and in the shadow of the very places where the American Revolution was born, there is an authenticity and immediacy to the experience that is breathtaking. *They were here:* Franklin, Jefferson, Adams, and Washington. And now, you are here.

It's both engaging and educational. Kids of all ages seem to love it, and Whoopi Goldberg has recorded a version of the story suitable for the younger ones. The tale of the founding fathers and mothers is dramatic, and the presentation takes advantage of the events. In one act, the audience is caught in the crossfire as British troops bear down on the Americans. This is visceral history. It hits you in the heart and in the head, and you can't help cheering and even shedding a tear or two as you watch the story of the Revolution unfold. It's also reasonably priced, at $17.76 per person, in 2004.

In Independence Park and Yosemite, two of the most popular national parks, and at Capulin, one of the most obscure national monuments, we made family memories that will last a lifetime, the kind of memories that ache to be shared. I will want to share Capulin with my grandchildren. My son will want to share Yosemite with his children. That's characteristic of the national parks. Like fairs, they appeal to all generations, and they naturally lend themselves to the creation of family traditions. Most kids love traditions, and so do their parents and grandparents. When you were a kid, weren't there some holiday rituals that you absolutely had to carry out or it just wouldn't be a proper Christmas or Passover? On summer vacation, when you were traveling by car with your folks, didn't you insist that you stop at Howard Johnson's or Stuckey's or Nickerson Farms? Didn't you love going to that special campsite—*your* campsite—in the national or regional park or forest or beach in the next state? Family tradition is a powerful emotional force on which many attraction operators can draw in their marketing, especially if they're willing and able to take the long view of their business.

It's clear from the research I've done that Moms everywhere are looking for memorable family entertainment options. It's also clear that for many of them, experiencing nature in some way is high on that list. For example, I gave my survey respondents two opportunities to let me know the places that are tops on their lists for family entertainment. I asked them to tell me where they would spend a week-end if the schedule were clear and price were no object. I also asked them to tell about their favorite family outing. Seven out of ten listed a state or national park, the beach, the river, camping, or another outdoor activity as a top choice. But what's more interesting is why they made the choices they did. Many said simply that these experiences offered something for everyone in the family. Others talked about cre-ating memories for their children. Some emphasized the educational opportunities that a natural setting provides. Overall, there was a feeling that nature, in all its guises, offered relaxation, refreshment, and renewal for the whole family. No tickets to buy, no lines to stand in, no traffic, no snarling hordes, no overwrought credit cards—in other words, a true vacation.

Attractions in Your Own Backyard

Good family entertainment is sometimes as close as your own backyard. In this post-9/11 world, more of us are looking close to home for those authentic and memo-rable experiences, and there are some wonderful surprises out there. Those feelings of wonder and delight—and never underestimate the power of a strong feeling—can kick in at some very unexpected places.

Take Vineland, Colorado, as an example. In October 2004, the Pantaleo Farm[8] hosted the fourth annual Great Pumpkin Patch by Moonlight Festival. For years through the 1990s, the Pantaleo family had opened their farm to schoolchildren and allowed them to come during the day to pick pumpkins. Then in 2001, they decid-ed to expand and allow families to come at night. That year the patch was open just one night, and over 2,500 people showed up! Who could resist picking a pumpkin under the light of the moon or by kerosene lamplight? The Pantaleos also offered hayrides, food, and a bonfire.

In year two, the family expanded the nighttime outings to three and added a costume contest, pony rides, craft vendors, and a giant corn maze. The attendance increased to 20,000—many from out of town. And that's in a region where the largest city is Pueblo, with approximately 98,000 inhabitants. Vineland is a tiny farming community with fewer than 5,000 people! Mr. Pantaleo and Walt Disney would have understood each other. Both succeeded in creating immersive experiences that could be enjoyed by all generations. In 2003, the Pantaleos did it again and the success grew. Of course, now it is a family tradition for many, and as long as the Pantaleos keep it authentic, they will continue to attract a large and lively audience.

In my little neighborhood, there's a different kind of family attraction called the Coffee Gallery. It's a coffeehouse that supports young artists by showcasing their works, and on weekends, it offers a wide variety of music and comedy acts on the Backstage. It's a great place for families. Imagine being able to take your children to see and hear world-class musicians in an intimate setting without fear of drunks or other distractions. The place has a wonderful attitude toward entertainment. "The policy of the Coffee Gallery Backstage is to present 'broadcast television clean' entertainment suitable for everyone. This is to ensure that the material will be of the highest quality and will come from 'thinking it through' instead of going for the cheap laugh. You may bring your brain with you. All ages welcomed."[9]

Owners Bob Stane (founder of the famed Ice House comedy club in Pasadena, California) and Ken Marshall have managed to create an environment that is warm and welcoming. They like families. They HAVE families. They are very involved in the community. Ken's kids play Little League, and he supports community programs both as a dad and as a business. In fact, for two years in a row, my husband used their Backstage area for his Little League get-acquainted meeting because it was raining.

In the coffeehouse, they provide toys for the kids to play with, books you can borrow to read and return, paintings and photographs to look at, a meeting room you can use for free as long as you reserve it, and great coffeehouse fare. It's about being good neighbors and giving good neighbors a chance to get together. That attitude creates a tremendous amount of loyalty and is beyond price.

Listen to Your Mother

The events of 9/11 gave all of us good reason to rethink our priorities. No story more poignantly pointed up the need to put family first than that of Howard Lutnick, the CEO of Cantor-Fitzgerald. On September 11, he lost 658 colleagues in his company. Only 120 survived. Lutnick himself missed the terrorist attack because he was taking his son to his first day of kindergarten. In the aftermath of the disaster, he promised that the company would take care of the families of those employees who had died. In fact, the remaining employees decided that their main reason for continuing to work was to take care of those families. The firm has pledged 25 percent of its profits over the next five years to a fund dedicated to that purpose. Lutnick's personal pain in losing his brother, his friends, and his colleagues gave a voice to all of us, and we hugged our families tighter after that chilling day. Lutnick acknowledged that the reward of focusing narrowly on work suddenly was not worth the cost of taking our families for granted.

Leisure travel, too, changed that day, and rekindled the desire to reach out to family and friends. The domestic terrorist alerts, unrest overseas, and the war in Iraq continue to keep folks on edge, especially about traveling by plane far from home. Even now, women—including the Moms who make the vast majority of travel plans for families—continue to be far more concerned about terrorism than men. The result: 70 percent of families who vacationed in 2002 decided it was time for a road trip.[10] They wanted quality time with their immediate family and a chance to visit relatives, enjoy outdoor activities, and visit national parks and monuments. The trend continued into 2003 and will undoubtedly persist—at least until the world situation and the economy stabilize. But there is a possibility that the new commitment to spending time with the family as our number-one priority will last way beyond the latest trend. These authentic experiences with friends and relatives—boating on the lake, camping in the national park, skiing in the mountains, or swimming in the ocean—will be memorable and worth repeating. And once something has been repeated, it's well on its way to becoming a tradition.

The best family attraction can be as large as Cirque du Soleil or as small as the Panteleo Farm. It can be as glorious as Yosemite or Yellowstone National Park or as surprising as Capulin Mountain. Certainly, it needs bathrooms, reasonable prices, places to rest, and fun activities. But even more than those, a great family attraction—the kind that becomes a well-loved tradition—speaks to the ageless heart.

Endnotes

1. Eric Minton, online at www.gettheloop.com.

2. www.iaapa.org.

3. www.wonderlandpark.com.

4. *Zumanity*, Cirque's new adult-oriented production, is the exception among the company's attractions; it is no doubt just as magical, but suited only for Mom and Dad.

5. www.fairsandexpos.com/history.aspx.

6. www.bigtex.com/history.html.

7. National Park Service, *Statistical Abstract, 2003*. Available online at www2.nature.nps.gov/stats/abst2003.pdf.

8. www.pantaleofarms.com.

9. www.coffeegallery.com.

10. Information on both terrorism and road trips is from the online survey conducted by Autobytel Inc., reported in *Columbus Wired*, June 2002, www.columbuswired.net. A 1999 Simmons Market Research survey (*American Demographics*, May 1999) found that only 43 percent of Americans vacationed by car. Thus, the 2002 figure represents a substantial increase over 1999.

Chapter 5

Theme Parks: A World Away—
Just Make Sure There Are
Enough Benches!

"One of our first family outings after arriving here from the East Coast," recalls Peter, "was to the recently opened Disneyland. As a boomer, I had been immersed in the Mickey Mouse Club, Davy Crockett, Mike Fink, and all the other aspects of the Disney mythology. I was as thrilled as a nine-year-old could be to actually visit the Magic Kingdom. Walking down Main Street in the park, my Dad said it was built like some of the towns back East that he remembered as a boy growing up.

"Forty years later, I am walking down that same Main Street with my two young daughters—not recalling the American towns that Walt and my father knew as children—but recalling the memory of being here with my Dad, as a young boy. And herein is the essential genius of Walt's dream: Disney markets experiences that are personal, memorable, and authentic. Moreover, they transcend generations and cultures around the world."

Peter nailed it, and here are the statistics that prove his point: Theme park and amusement park spending is expected to recover from the 9/11 downturn and grow between now and 2008, driven by the opening of new parks, improvements to old parks, and a much stronger economy. So says PricewaterhouseCoopers in its *Global*

Entertainment and Media Outlook: 2004–2008. In addition, visitor demographics will shift. Currently, half of park visitors are in the 25- to 44-year-old range. Over the next five years, that group will be trounced by the 45- to 64-year-olds! Older Moms (and younger grandmoms) with time and money will be arranging for vacations for their tweens, teens, and grandkids, assuring that the family traditions will live on in the next generation!

It is not my intention to review all theme parks in this book, but rather to draw some conclusions about the industry as a whole based on a sample of major players in California and Florida, where many of those players are concentrated. I want to examine how successful a few parks have been in their mission to attract families, and determine what they do, or ought to do, to catch the eye—and the purse—of Moms. Disney did it first and, by most accounts, still does it best, so it seems the best place to start. In fact, it simply isn't possible to talk about family entertainment or the Mom Factor without talking about Disney.

Disney: The Mostly Model 600-Pound Gorill . . .er, Mouse

Walt Disney almost single-handedly invented the idea of a destination family entertainment experience. "The voyage that ended with the opening of Disneyland in 1955 really began when Walt was entertaining his little girls on Sundays in the early 1940s," according to the Disney biography *The Man Behind the Magic.* "As the children took their 15th ride around the merry-go-round, Walt would sit quietly on a wooden bench, wondering why no one had invented a clean, safe place where parents and children could enjoy themselves at the same time."[1] *Imagine that!* A place where parents and children could have fun! Whatever you think of the House of Mouse today, Disneyland, and then Disney World and most of the rest of Disney's properties, have fulfilled that promise handsomely.

Given Disney's history, I should not have been surprised at how many of the southern California Moms who took my survey owned season passes to Disneyland. Lawrie, the mother of five (four girls and one boy), chooses the Disney experience to top her list of family entertainment favorites. She lives in southern California, but loves taking her kids to EPCOT in Florida, and always has. "I've always tried to get my kids to recognize the beauty around them. I like taking them places that are 'almost educational.' I feel like the things they see at EPCOT help them to be more open-minded about the world. I love it and so do they—even the littlest one has a great time. That's not to say we don't occasionally go for the thrills and spills of a Six Flags, because we do. But *my* favorite place is EPCOT."

Part of the joy of Disneyland and Disney World for Moms like Lawrie and dads like Peter comes from sharing the dreams and experiences of their youth with their own children. Disney understands the value of the shared memory. In 2002, I started seeing commercials that focused on grandparents taking their grandchildren to Disneyland, a sure indication that the idea of multigenerational memories had taken hold. Then, as if to confirm it, I had a conversation with my optometrist. She's a wonderful woman on the far side of 50, and she has grandchildren she adores. We were talking about the *Mom Factor* and she said, "Your next book should be the *Grandmom Factor*. Here I am, at a time in my life when I have more money and more time than ever before. I want to find fun things to do with my grandchildren, and the only company that I get information from is Disney! They sent me info on their cruises, and I think that's what I'm going to do with my grandkids."

Contrary to current practice across much of the entertainment industry, Walt Disney did not carry out finely tuned focus group studies or charrettes to determine what would make the most people happy. Quite the opposite: The early Disney magic was based on Walt's intuition. Whatever it told him, I'm glad he listened. His park set the standard for the rest of the industry in characteristics such as cleanliness, friendliness, safety, and attention to detail, all of which are important to Moms. But those things alone wouldn't have been enough to build the Disney parks empire. Walt managed two other feats that made his creation a prominent continuing feature of the American pop-culture landscape.

First, he transported young and old to places that once lived only in our imaginations. For many years, Disneyland was the only place where a childhood fantasy (even if you were already grown-up) took corporeal form. Children and former children from Maine to Florida, Washington to Texas dreamed of going there (helped along, of course, by Disney television programming). The castle, the characters, the music on Main Street, flying with Dumbo or Peter Pan, paddling through piratical plunder, shrieking with glee at the happy haunts suddenly sitting between you and your Mom: at Disneyland, stories came to life, and Disney has always been all about story. Not just any story, either. Walt knew how to touch our hearts, with patriotic pride in Mr. Lincoln, nostalgia at the soda fountain or nickelodeon, the thrill of island exploration in a coonskin cap, the futuristic wonder of monorail travel. So much of Disneyland resonated emotionally with visitors that many felt a genuine fondness for the place. It wasn't just "I sure had fun there," but "I love that place! Can we pleeeeeease go back?"

Walt's second feat goes back to what Lawrie emphasized: *She* likes Disney's EPCOT. She would go there *without* her children. It amazes and engages *her*! That is a very important lesson to be learned from Disney. As Stitch says in *Lilo and Stitch*, "Ohana means family. Family means no one is left behind or forgotten." Not even Mom.

Moms have a tendency to make choices for the family without much regard for themselves. There are whole libraries of literature on the giving nature of mothers. When I was growing up, my mother fried chicken about once a week. There were four of us and we all had our favorite pieces. Dad wanted a breast, my brother wanted a leg, and I took the thigh. My mother always said her favorite piece was the back. It took me a long time to figure out that it was her favorite piece because it was all that was left! She let everyone else get what they wanted before she made a choice. That happens in dozens of ways every week in every family in America. Moms take what's left. Imagine, then, the power of creating a destination attraction where Moms don't feel as though they are an afterthought. That is part of the enduring attractiveness of Disneyland and the other Disney parks. Moms are entertained there. And just so we don't lose sight of why that's significant for the industry, please keep in mind that women make 90 percent of the vacation plans for families,[2] which translates into billions of dollars annually.

Just what does Disney do that's attractive to Mom? To begin with, Mom is just like the rest of the girls—she likes to shop when she's on vacation. Yes, you can buy every imaginable piece of Disneyana, but other choices abound. With 50 stores at Disneyland alone—from Madhatters to Gag Factory/Toon Town Five and Dime to Jewel of Orleans to Bonanza Outfitters—there are opportunities for much more than Mickey T-shirts, Goofy ears, and Minnie dolls. You'll find everything from baseball hats and whoopee cushions to estate jewelry, authentic Hawaiian shirts, and lovely carved wooden boxes. Prices are not bargain-basement, but neither are they heart-attack high. In addition to a wide selection and mostly reasonable prices, each store is fun just to walk through. My favorite shopping area at Disneyland is New Orleans Square. The shops there are really different from those in most theme parks and not over-burdened with cheap souvenir Mickeys and Minnies. Instead, I browse through fine crystal sculptures and glassware, magic tricks, hand painted parasols, and antiques—and then I can get my son's portrait done in pastels if I want. It's an altogether charming shopping experience.

Disney parks also feature live music. We all know that music hath charms to soothe the savage beast. If Mom is stuck waiting outside Space Mountain while the kids ride that roller coaster for the fourth time, she can *sit* (very important to Mom, Grandmom, and other patient adults) and often listen to a good live band. When she is entertained, she's not looking at her watch, fidgeting, and looking forward to getting out of there.

Disney has always been good about offering a variety of food, and to prove it is in tune with the times, the parks have added a nice selection of healthy choices. The prices are high, but not so high that we resent it. In fact, I always try to get reservations at the Blue Bayou, undoubtedly the most expensive restaurant in Disneyland—but also the most beautiful! It has actual table service instead of self-service, and Moms love to be waited on. We hardly ever find that option at a theme park. If you are (or have ever watched) a Mom with three kids in tow trying to eat at a place where you have to slide trays down a serving line, you will understand how frustrating it can be to attempt to take care of the individual needs of each child. Often they can't take their own trays, so Mom has to double or triple up. One false move and you've got a disaster on your hands—or on the floor. So being able to sit down and have someone else tend to the service makes the meal into something Mom is much more likely to enjoy and not just endure. Of course, it also turns a meal into a memory worth repeating.

Now here's something that might be perceived as simpleminded by many in my audience: Disneyland and Disney World are pretty. I love the landscaping. It's a joy just to stroll through the grounds! And it's not just me. Babette, who has an annual Disneyland pass for her family of four, mentioned the joys of just sitting with her youngest and watching the ducks, looking at the flowers and relaxing. Lest this point skate by those of you interested in the Mom demographic, let me emphasize: She's willing to pay a lot of money for the opportunity to *sit*.

Finally, let's look briefly at the individual attractions within the parks. Disneyland and Disney World really were designed as places where "parents *and* children could have fun." The Haunted House, Pirates of the Caribbean, and other dark rides are rich enough experiences to delight people of all ages. Even the roller coasters are wild enough for most kids and tame enough for most Moms. *I have never felt that my only purpose in accompanying my family to Disneyland was to hand out money and hold everybody's jackets.* I, the Mom, look forward to going there—and I can't overemphasize how important that observation is, or ought to be, for theme park designers and operators.

Now, quickly, before I'm accused of working for the Mouse (I'm one of the few I know in the leisure entertainment industry who never has), I want to point out that even Disney can miscalculate. It's not all peaches and cream.

California Adventure, the newest of the Disney parks, opened next to Disneyland in February 2001. With it, Disney sought to capture kids a bit older than those who went with their folks to Disneyland. Reviews from industry experts and from the press have been mixed at best, despite some design tweaks along the way. A recent trip to the park, with two teenagers serving as guinea pigs, reiterated why. As we left, I asked the kids to rate California Adventure and Disneyland. Disneyland won hands down, with an eight on a scale of one to ten, while California Adventure got only a four. The reason, explained Francesca, a 14-year-old, was that "there's so much more to do at Disneyland than just ride rides." Out of the mouths of babes. It seems that Disney did almost the opposite of what it had hoped to do—attract teenagers. It managed to jumble things in a way that made this theme park much less appealing than Disneyland to teens *and* to Moms, especially those steeped in the Disney tradition. You know all those Moms in my survey who had season passes to Disneyland? Not one of them had a pass to California Adventure. Let's explore the reasons.

First of all, California Adventure has no hook. If you go to the Hollywood Pictures Backlot–area of the park, you can see a short movie on the life of Walt Disney. In it, Walt makes it very explicit that he decided to use the medium of television to promote his theme park. And he did it well. The *Wonderful World of Color* was a Sunday night ritual in millions of homes across America. That television show made sure that practically every kid in America hoped to go to Disneyland someday. It was only in Disneyland that they could see their favorite characters and experience a fantasy come true. There truly was no place else on earth quite like it.

California Adventure, on the other hand, doesn't have that advantage. It isn't a place with its own built-in well-known identity. It is a tagalong baby brother—cute, but often annoying. Moms, who crave good stories and authentic experiences for their kids, see a bit too much of Las Vegas in California Adventure. Yes, it does attempt to create authentic experiences, but by *re*-creating authentic places inauthentically. I know a lot of the world thinks that California is a fantasyland, and I'll admit there's some truth to that. But putting a Napa Valley Winery, Santa Monica's Pier, Monterey's Cannery Row, and San Francisco's Golden Gate Bridge into a park where all those very real places are within a day's drive left me feeling short-changed. It would have made more sense to build a Paris-themed park for Californians. And the kids didn't even notice that the different areas were themed. What they wanted was shorter lines, lots more thrill rides, and cool things to look at on the walks between rides.

If one reason for creating California Adventure was to appeal to an older demographic, then the boat was not only missed, it might have sunk. On a Sunday in May, the park was certainly crowded, but not nearly to capacity, and it was full of baby strollers, many double-wide. They were so numerous and reckless that my son suggested they needed a stroller lane complete with stoplights and pedestrian crossings. Most of the stroller crowd wound up in the newest section of the park—A Bug's Life. Notice that the California theme was abandoned once the Disney brass figured out that, even though they weren't supposed to, families with small children were coming to the park and going home disappointed, because there wasn't enough for the little ones to do. On the day I was there, the six-and-under crowd clearly outnumbered the 12-and-older crowd. Disney's attempts to appeal to Moms and dads also failed that day—the winery, the bakery, and the tortilla factory areas were almost deserted. On the other hand, the lines were long at the Grizzly River Run, by far the most popular ride in the park, probably because it and the California Screamin' roller coaster were the only true thrill rides. Recognizing a need, Disney opened a new thrill ride for this park in the summer of 2004 called The Twilight Zone Tower of Terror, bringing the number of thrill rides up by a whopping 50 percent!

Shopping was a real letdown, too, especially when compared with Disneyland. Every store I popped into had almost identical merchandise, and most of it was the typical souvenir-keychain-stuffed-toy-T-shirt-goofy-hat variety. There was music, though never enough and not in the places that would have made my wait-time fly. The employees seemed less well trained than their Disneyland counterparts. The landscaping was much less imaginative and featured much more concrete than at Disneyland; there were hardly any trees except on the perimeter of the park, and shade was hard to come by.

There were a few bright spots. One was the Fast Pass system (also available at Disneyland and DisneyWorld), which gives you an appointment at an express-line entrance for the most popular rides. If we had a Fast Pass ticket, it cut the wait in line by two-thirds or more. (However, it seemed impossible to figure out how to schedule all the must-do rides on the Fast Pass. I assume that is by design. It can't be all Fast Pass all the time, or we're back to the same length line.) In addition, the park and its bathrooms were very clean, though the bathroom lines were very long. Finally, I felt that my teens were perfectly safe running off by themselves.

Okay, I know that Disney did not design California Adventure to be a mere clone of Disneyland. It was designed to be different. Nonetheless, as a Mom used to the joys of a day at Disneyland, I found that California Adventure just doesn't meet my expectations. Moms like me who go once are unlikely to make the return trip. Nor, clearly, does it attract the hordes of teenagers Disney wanted. There's a great park across the way that's more fun for both parents and teens, as well as kids under 12. So what should Disney do?

From the standpoint of the Mom Factor, Moms would appreciate better staff training, a wider variety of shopping, more thoughtful placement of musicians, more creative landscaping, more shady spots, and a more appealing presentation of grownup experiences. But solving the fundamental problem of inauthenticity would require revamping the theme entirely, an unlikely course of action in any case. If we assume that the goal of this park is still to attract teens, then maybe making things better for Moms, while helpful, should not be the only focus. (Yes, that was me you heard saying that.) A better approach might be to reposition the park explicitly as the teen destination at Disneyland, and include California Adventure in the price of a Disneyland ticket (a move Disney made during the spring and summer of 2004), at least at some price levels. Add more thrill rides à la Six Flags (again, the Tower of Terror is a move in that direction) since conventional wisdom in the industry says that teenagers prefer great thrill rides to the often gentler pleasures of Disneyland. The thrill-seekers in the family could take off for California Adventure with their walkie-talkies. The traditionalists and the rest of the group could head for the Magic Kingdom. The two groups could meet in Downtown Disney for lunch, dinner or the parade that night. Moms would feel good about letting the older ones roam in either park because they know their kids are safe. If, as Walt suggested, the Magic Kingdom will never be finished, then maybe this scenario isn't entirely a fantasy.

What Makes a Theme Park a Theme Park?

The troubles of California Adventure notwithstanding, Disneyland and its siblings have been so successful over the last 50 years that they have spawned a host of imitators. Today, over 600 theme and amusement parks and attractions dot the United States, with one within a two-hour drive of every major metropolitan area. The variety of theme parks alone is astonishing, as a few examples will demonstrate. Dollywood in Pigeon Forge, Tennessee, has a Smoky Mountain/Dolly Parton's life theme. There are crafts, a working gristmill, thrill rides, water rides, a good dose of history in the Robert F. Thomas Chapel (come to Sunday services), and the Southern Gospel Music Hall of Fame. The park even has a preserve for non-releasable bald eagles. Hersheypark in Hershey, Pennsylvania, is America's only chocolate-themed park. It boasts more than 60 rides and attractions, live shows, shopping, and dining. And of course, chocolate. Not only can you eat it, learn about it, see it made, and smell it everywhere, at the Spa at the Hotel Hershey you can get the Whipped Cocoa Bath, the Cocoa Butter Scrub, and the Chocolate FondueWrap. (Every time I eat chocolate, I think, "I might as well just apply it to my thighs." And that's exactly what they do—only it's good for you!) A Mom's idea of heaven on earth! Then there's Silver Dollar City in Branson, Missouri, underneath which you can explore gigantic Marvel Cave; and the Enchanted Forest in Salem, Oregon, where you can visit a 17th-century European village; and Buffalo Bill's in Jean, Nevada, where you can ride the Western-themed coaster or let it ride at the craps table.

Given the variety of parks out there, it might be useful to revisit in more detail the difference between theme parks and amusement parks. Part of the distinction has to do with building great people places on the strength of a trusted, or at the very least, a well-known, brand. Part of it has to do with storytelling in an immersive environment. Media companies are naturals for theme parks because they have well-known stories to tell in new ways. Universal Studios, Warner Bros. Studios, and Paramount Studios all got into the business by repackaging their stable of hit properties or by buying well-established parks and bringing in characters. Universal Studios uses its huge movie library and its old studio tour as the theme for its parks. Warner Bros., which used to own Six Flags before it sold its theme park business to Premier Parks, used its animated characters to establish a theme. (Premier now licenses those characters and the rights to the movie-themed rides.) Paramount Studios entered the park business with a different idea in mind. The characters that you find at its parks are mostly from Nickelodeon. The parks reflect little of Paramount's tremendous film library. (The attractions side of the house provides a counterpoint: Paramount owns and operates Star Trek: The Experience at the Las Vegas Hilton. In fact, it expanded the popular attraction in 2004, with a 4D movie starring the dreaded Borg.) Disney MGM Studios brings together former competitors with very different movie libraries, and offers guests everything from Twilight Zone and Indiana Jones to Muppets and Little Mermaids.

The fundamental difference for me is really quite simple—to be a theme park you need a theme. Six Flags fails that test, although it comes up in Internet searches for theme parks *or* amusement parks. The original Six Flags Over Texas in Arlington had rides and attractions designed and named to reflect each of the six flags that had flown over Texas: Spain, Mexico, France, the Republic of Texas, the

United States, and the Confederacy. When the company expanded and started naming other parks Six Flags, they tried to retain the flag theme for a while, but soon
the idea faded away. The "theme" at most Six Flags parks today, such as it is,
amounts to the use of licensed comic-book and animated characters such as
Superman and Bugs Bunny, with barely a nod to the story or the context. These
parks are, according to my definition, amusement parks. That's not a bad thing. It
just means the emphasis is different, and I believe the audience is, too.

Some Challengers to the Mouse

Legoland. Legoland in Carlsbad, California, has emerged as a great family theme
park. Danish toy company Lego has used its ubiquitous building blocks as the foundation of the park's theme. They are everywhere—even as part of the employee's uniforms. The park has always attracted a younger crowd, with toddlers to ten-year-olds
reigning. It has many of the attributes of a Mom haven. It's clean and beautifully
landscaped. Miniland USA is a remarkable assemblage of iconic American buildings—all built with Legos—and it alone is almost worth the price of admission! It's
educational, with multiple opportunities to build with Legos and discover some
basic laws of physics and engineering. In the summer of 2003, the park went all out
to attract a slightly older crowd by opening the Legoland Sports Jam and the Sports
Center, featuring extreme sports as well as basketball, baseball, soccer, and more. It
expanded on this theme in 2004 and has even made a concerted effort to do something special for girls. Lego has introduced a new line of toys called Clikits that girls
can use to design jewelry, picture frames, and hair and fashion accessories. They can
test the new toys and shake hands with Clikits girls making the rounds of the park.

Moving to attract more girls is a good move for Lego. I remember offering to
take my son to Legoland for his tenth birthday. He was jazzed about it until he
mentioned it to two of his friends. Both of them had been to the park and both gave
it a very knowing "thumbs down." Both of them were girls. Their influence was
enough to keep him from choosing the park as his birthday destination. Clearly,
reaching out to young girls has since become a priority for the company and for
the park.

The Lego marketing people seem to understand the importance of Mom in the
ticket-buying process. They organized the Legoland Model Mom Club for Moms
with children four and under. Club members get a one-year pass for $42 that is good
only on Thursday mornings. The offerings include stroller fitness, play groups, and
lectures by childhood experts, along with free run of the park. The program is obvi-

ously for the local Moms, and what a way to get and keep their loyalty while creating a lifetime of wonderful memories! Dads, grandparents, and other caregivers are also encouraged to come—although you may purchase only one Mom Club membership per family.

Knott's Berry Farm. It's funny to some, but I put Knott's Berry Farm on the theme park list. Its history reaches back to the 1920s, when Walter and Cordelia Knott sold their boysenberries (he bred the first of that species) at a roadside stand. Cordelia decided to open a restaurant, and Walter decided to put in a few fun things to amuse folks while they were waiting for dinner. He chose an Old West theme, and to this day, you can still pan for gold and get caught in a staged gunfight and train robbery. By the 1990s, the park had added not just roller coasters and thrill rides, but Mystery Lodge, in which an Indian storyteller captures guests' imaginations by telling Native American tales in a magical setting. Here, among the death-defying coasters, there's still a bit of Old West education going on. The park no longer belongs to the Knott family. But under Cedar Fair ownership, it still offers many things Moms look for: a beautiful and comfortable setting (there's lots of shade here from well-established trees), engagement on many levels, and a variety of attractions, from thrill rides to those bits of Old West history and mythology. Camp Snoopy is the theme of the park section designed for the little-bittys. Snoopy and Woodstock rule this roost, and it was there that my child, just like thousands of other southern California children, rode his first roller coaster. The food throughout the park is good, varied, and reasonable, by theme-park standards. You can still buy Cordelia's fried chicken dinner. I even enjoy shopping there because I can buy fossilized trilobites and high-quality cowboy hats. There's lots of music and color and true family fun. Although not many teens will admit it, they enjoy the park precisely because it's a little corny—they look back with nostalgia on the days when they were little kids here—and yet there are enough thrill rides to satisfy most of them. And there is simply no scarier place to go at Halloween than Knott's Scary Farm.

Sea World and Discovery Cove. If Disney's Animal Kingdom in Florida is a theme park with a zoo theme, Sea World is a theme park with an ocean and aquarium theme. Originally, it was all marine animals, aquariums, and shows. Today, all the parks also boast thrill rides and playgrounds, 4D theaters, and simulator rides. They are a most interesting mix of marine biology, showmanship, education, and entertainment. And I have to admit, it works for me. Today, Busch Entertainment Corporation, one of beer-maker Anheuser Busch's many companies, owns all three Sea World parks. Sea World San Diego was the first. It opened its doors in March

1964 and, since then, has seen 100 million visitors pass through its gates.[3] The other Sea World parks are in San Antonio and Orlando.

What makes Sea World so wonderful is that it offers a rare and precious experience—direct contact with a variety of sea life. You can touch sea stars (the creatures formerly known as starfish) and sea cucumbers, feed sea lions and dolphins, or run your hand over a ray's back. The park even provides a place to wash the fishy stuff off your hands when your dolphin food is all gone. For an additional fee, you can take a behind-the-scenes tour and touch a penguin or a shark, or, if that's not a close enough encounter, you can snorkel or scuba dive with sharks. Or interact in the water with false killer whales. Want even more? You can pay $200 or more and be a trainer for a day. It doesn't surprise me that Sea World just keeps adding interaction possibilities, that it can charge so much, nor that it has lots of takers. An experience that allows a child or even a jaded Mom to get so close to such magnificent creatures can be life-changing. It's unique, immersive (literally), and memorable. That makes the money a secondary consideration. The popularity of such encounters inspired Busch to create a whole new kind of theme park, and I predict there will be many imitators.

Discovery Cove, adjacent to Sea World in Orlando, is a cross between a water park and an aquarium. Only here, the guests see everything from the fish's point of view. The centerpiece attraction is an opportunity to swim with the dolphins. But you can also hand-feed exotic birds and snorkel with exotic fish and rays. You can float down a tropical river and stare down sharks and barracudas. You get everything you need—a mask, a snorkel, towels, sunscreen, a meal, parking, a photo—for a single price at the country's first reservations-only theme park. That's right, there is a cap on the number of people allowed in the park on a given day. That's why prices start at $130 and go up to $400 per person, depending on how intense an experience you want. It's like renting a tropical island for the day for your family.

This kind of experience, not unlike parts of Animal Kingdom, is family-friendly, affordable ecotourism. You can't or don't want to take your family to Belize. Instead, you can choose Discovery Cove, where the close encounters are assured and in a safe and controlled environment. They feel very exciting, even a little dangerous, and yet there's no chance of actually being bitten by a shark, no worries about the drinking water or the plumbing, no chance of coming home empty-handed. These environmental experiences in their own way mirror the attraction of roller coasters and other thrill rides: all the adrenalin and none of the risk of actually jumping out of a plane or riding over a waterfall or rocketing into space.

Sea World and Discovery Cove are favorites with Moms for all the Disney reasons and many more. The possibility of a life-changing encounter is as appealing to her as to the kids. The educational content at these parks is unbeatable. Every attraction has a knowledgeable trainer with a good script informing us about the walruses or the Beluga whales or even the snails and crabs. The interactive exhibits around the various enclosures are usually quite informative and full of things kids can do to discover or demonstrate certain scientific principles. Even the bathrooms are large and usually clean. The parks are beautiful, enchanting places to visit. In fact, the only downside I can see (and it applies only to Sea World proper, not to Discovery Cove) is the quality of the food—only fair, especially considering theme-park prices. I guess nobody is perfect.

Listen to Your Mother

On the whole, theme parks stack up as pretty good family entertainment, if you can afford them. Face it, a day at Disneyland or Sea World or almost any park can be very expensive for a family of four, especially if you include hotel, food, and gas or airline tickets. That's one of the reasons that most people go to Disneyland only rarely, unless they live close enough to make a season pass pay or take advantage of zip-code discounts. You can always tell when the attendance at a theme park is not up to expectations because the discount offers for the local population multiply. Suffice it to say that 2003 was a good year for theme-park aficionados who live in southern California because the post-9/11 economic doldrums persisted.

However, "if you huff and puff and finally save enough money up to take your family on a trip" to any of the major American theme parks, then it's hard to have a really bad time. They have done a reasonably good job of fulfilling the Mom Factor requirements, partly because they had such a good example to follow. There were no theme parks in the United States until 1955.[4] Once the theme park was invented, and once it was a proven success, the public placed high expectations on those entering the market, from the moment the doors opened.

Theme parks have become as American as apple pie and—dare I say it—as Mom. Keep them clean. Keep them safe. Keep them engaging and occasionally educational. Keep them beautiful. Keep them friendly. And chances are, I won't stress out about running up credit-card debt to make sure my family can make some memories together.

Endnotes

1. Katherine Barrett, Richard Greene, Katherine Greene, and N. Paulsen, *The Man Behind the Magic: The Story of Walt Disney* (New York: Viking, 1991).

2. Prerogative Marketing Consultancy, www.prerog.com.

3. Sea World news release, April 30, 2004.

4. Amusement parks have had a much longer and more dangerous past life; see National Amusement Park Historical Association, www.napha.org.

Chapter 6

Sports: It's Not a Guy Thing Anymore

Let me tell you a little story about the Queen of Baseball. I never watched a baseball game in my life until my Mom got me going to games in Dodgers Stadium at the ripe old age of 35. And if I was going to go, so was my husband and her husband. (For my stepdad, though, it was just a courtesy. He always took a book to the stadium and read during the game.) Sharing her love of the game was part of the Queen's magic.

Others have disputed her claim to the title of Queen, but their counterclaims are spurious. Only the real Queen could have turned her love of baseball into a little boy's passion. When I was pregnant with her grandson, the Queen would take us to ball games. It was the perfect outing for a pregnant lady. Good (junk) food, cool nights, and wide seats. It was clear early on that this little boy growing inside me was a Dodgers fan. How he would kick and fuss when he heard those Mets fans misbehaving! We still tease him about it. Some of his first words were, "Ed-die! Ed-die!" (to encourage first baseman Eddie Murray). Today, that same little boy has finished seven years of Little League, with five All-Star trophies, and two years of Pony League ball, and is hoping to make his high school team. No one else in the family ever played baseball. No one else in the family ever had a tiddlywink's worth of athletic ability. The Queen made it so.

And the little boy's passion became his father's. The Queen would be so proud of her son-in-law. He coached or managed a Little League team every year for six years. One loyal fan begat four more. She always felt that baseball was somehow a great metaphor for life. It went way beyond the idea of winning and losing. It had to do with teamwork and fun and persistence and fun and loyalty and fun and being outside and fun. But I have to tell you, she really hated the bathrooms at Dodgers Stadium.

I'd like to point out that my mother was directly responsible for ticket sales, hotdog and T-shirt purchases, and book sales—not just for one grandma, but for five fans—and trust me, she was never the only granny in the stands.

So sports are not always a guy thing. Sometimes sports are a girl thing, even a grandma thing. And sports are definitely a family entertainment thing. Professional sports are a multibillion-dollar industry and, we assume, an American birthright. But in the last few years, profits have been slipping in the major sports. In July 2002, journalist Eric Fisher observed, it was clear that Major League Baseball was in trouble, with attendance down in midseason and a strike looming. Major League Soccer folded teams. Long-planned stadium projects in five major cities were canceled or put on hold. Television ratings were down across the board. The National Basketball Association had been relegated to cable, even with Michael Jordan coming and going. Why such disarray? Fisher attributed a significant part of this "industry downturn" to:

> . . . *a broad lifestyle change among children and teenagers. Corporate dollars and adult fans are the primary economic drivers of sports today, but children are those of tomorrow and their interest in professional and major college sports is a fraction of what it was even a decade ago . . . . [M]any leagues and teams are investing unprecedented time and resources into grassroots marketing to win back one fan and one viewer at a time— literally.*[1]

The federal government estimated that, in 1997, there were 35 million kids from four to 18 years of age involved in organized sports in this country.[2] Almost 3 million are involved in Little League baseball and softball (along with a million adult volunteers). There are another 630,000 four- to 16-year-olds and 250,000 adult volunteers involved in American Youth Soccer Organization (AYSO) leagues—only one of many ways to participate in soccer—and 360,000 kids are signed up for Pop Warner football.[3] But these numbers don't reflect middle-school and high-school athletic teams. In the state of Texas alone, over 1 million middle-school and high-school kids participate in interscholastic-league sports.[4] These statistics are important because little football and baseball players are likely to become big football and baseball fans. It's right here that sports marketers will find the roots of that grass they are after.

So what's the key to reversing the decline? How do great sports fans from little T-ball players grow? I suggest you ask your mother.

Look at it this way: In general, Moms write the checks to sign up the kids for sports and take them to practice. Moms buy the uniforms, the special shoes, the team pictures, and the team snacks. Moms run most of the volunteer organizations, whether it's a pep club for the school basketball team or the board for the local Little League. Moms keep the family schedules to make sure that each and every child gets where the child is supposed to be when he or she is supposed to be there. Moms are the number one cheerleaders at every game, and they often coach as well. So Moms are intensely involved in sports at the most basic—grassroots—level.

But women's—and Mom's—love of sports doesn't stop with the Little League closing ceremonies. Let me share a few eye-opening statistics with you. In 1997, over 40 percent of the audience for all men's professional sports was women.[5] The expectation is that by 2030, 50 percent of the audience will be women. It's also estimated that today 43 percent of the National Football League's audience is female. The proportion is even higher for Major League Baseball. The National Hockey League attracts 33 percent women and the National Basketball Association reports 19 percent female fans. You add it all up and you get 50 million female pro-sports fans.[6] The importance of these figures is clear to the marketing professionals in the five major professional sports. In 1999, Major League Baseball officials commissioned a study, *Women and Baseball.* They learned (no surprise to readers of this book!) that mothers are the primary decision makers regarding most household matters, including leisure activities such as ball games. Baseball Commissioner Bud Selig figured this one out: "When I first became commissioner, I said that one of my goals was to put a bat and ball in the hands of every child. It seems that, for many kids, we first must put the right baseball stories in front of their Moms."[7]

Now he's talking my language. It is my contention that Moms are not only the key to ticket sales (no longer the primary source of income, by the way—TV revenues are), but the key to the television market, memorabilia and gear sales, and most important, the next generation of fans. I don't discount the influence of men on sports or the treasured American ideal of father and son in the ballpark on Sunday afternoon. I just want to point out that it's very likely that Mom is there, too, and that the whole thing was her idea. It has been an interesting journey to discover just how much influence Mom has on the sports industry, but it seems clear that women—and let's not forget, over three-quarters of the women in America are mothers—are changing the face of sports from the T-ball leagues to the pros.

The Houses That Ruth and the Rest Built

Let's start with the places in which professional sporting events occur. Stadium building was a booming business all through the 1990s. The economics of having a professional sports team in your hometown are pretty persuasive. According to Economics Research Associates, a team not only aids the local economy in measurable ways, it contributes intangibles, too: things such as civic pride, added entertainment choices, and higher profiles for cities with teams appear on the checklists of mayors and city council members everywhere. Consequently—even with some major cities putting their stadiums on hold—new stadiums are being planned and built in cities across America, many of them for minor league baseball teams. Some are attached to convention centers or are designated as family entertainment centers. The idea is to turn a stadium or arena into a place that can attract a wide demographic that comes earlier, stays longer, and even comes in the off-season.

A quick look at some of the innovations in the new sports cathedrals hints that this male-dominated business is beginning to understand the power of family, and maybe even the power of Mom.

In 1996, when Turner Field was converted from an Olympic stadium into the home of the Atlanta Braves, the first baseball theme park was born. Even then, Major League Baseball realized that fans wanted more of a baseball experience than a $4 hotdog and a $7 cold beer. Stadium owners realized that there was money to be made if a fan's stay at the park could be lengthened. Give fans a reason to come early and stay late and you'll be more successful. It's the same psychology that drives mall developers to add entertainment to shopping.

The Atlanta Braves organization hired Jack Rouse Associates to come up with some concepts for engaging the fans before and after the game. The original list included a whole series of interactive ways to test baseball skill levels at all ages. There were touch-screen kiosks for everything from scouting reports to testing your knowledge of baseball trivia. The stadium redesign included a Braves Museum and Hall of Fame and a new fancy restaurant. A children's play area called Tooner Field was installed. A day at the ballpark began to resemble a day at the amusement park, and that was the idea.

The project was successful enough to encourage most new and remodeled stadiums since then to pick up on some or all of its elements. One prime example of turning a ballpark into an all-day affair is the home of the Texas Rangers in Arlington, Texas. Included in the facility is a museum called Legends of the Game. Among its offerings are exhibits on baseball in general, and the Rangers and the Texas League in particular. It also offers educational programs and training for kids and teachers, using baseball as the common denominator to teach a wide variety of subjects. There are birthday party packages, storytime for little kids, after-school programs, and my personal favorite—sleepovers! Perfect for a Mom's Night Off!

When my son was very young and very energetic, we decided to try karate lessons. He had a wonderful teacher named Tom Serrano, whose rapport with the kids was terrific. He provided them with life lessons as well as lessons in karate. He also understood parents, and every two months or so, he would open the dojo for a sleepover. He charged $25, and that covered pizza for dinner and pancakes for breakfast. The kids practiced their karate, played games, and watched movies until they fell asleep. Tom and one or two other instructors provided the adult supervision. And Mom and Dad went out on the town. It was wonderful!

The Philadelphia Phillies organization, too, reached out to kids and parents in its old stadium, and continued this tradition when its new stadium opened in 2004. In an area of the park called Ashburn Alley, fans will find a retail store, a variety of food and drink options, and plenty of picnic tables. It opens two-and-a-half hours prior to weekday games and three hours before weekend games so fans can watch batting practice. This fun area spans the entire outfield concourse and includes All-Star Walk; Bullpens, where fans have the chance to view the bilevel bullpens and watch pitchers from both teams warm up; the Citizens Bank–sponsored Games of Baseball entertainment area that includes interactive games such as Run the Bases, Ballpark Pinball, and Pitch 'Em & Tip 'Em; and, finally, Memory Lane, an illustrated history of all Philadelphia baseball, including the Phillies, Philadelphia Athletics, and Negro League teams in the city. The intention is to offer "family-fun amenities, lively entertainment, and enhanced concessions."[8]

Now, I applaud all these innovations that add value and fun to a trip to the ballpark. Certainly more ways to entertain the kids will make the experience last longer and might indeed encourage more families to attend. But keep in mind that here, just as at most amusement parks, Moms are primarily cheerleaders and money machines. The least that we can expect is to be comfortable while we dish out support and dollars for the interactive games. That's why the picnic area and the museum parts of the Phillies experience appeal to me. And I love the idea of having a special place to watch the pitchers warm up and the rest of the team take batting practice.

I wonder if there are any little amenities just for Moms in any of the new stadiums being built across the country? I'm looking for things such as more restrooms designed to accommodate Moms with children in tow. (Not a bad idea for the men's rooms either.) The engineering problem of strollers and restrooms is a serious one and is finally beginning to get some attention.

I'd like to add a little side note to my constant chatter on proper bathroom facilities. When I have broached the subject of the women's bathroom mess with various men in positions of power—from architects to builders to owners—more often than not, I've heard, "Women are so hard on the plumbing!" I think that in their sensitive and politically correct way, they are trying to say they've had it with calling plumbers to dig sanitary napkins out of the toilets. Okay. That is a problem. But here's another one. At large gatherings is it not uncommon for women to spend ten minutes or more in line waiting for a stall. Quite often, Moms wait with wriggling children. By the time they actually get to the toilet, they are so angry at the line, the inefficiency, their children, and the pain in their bladders, that they just don't care about your plumbing. And I don't care how hard we women may occasionally be on the plumbing, we don't wet the seats, flood the floors, and corrode the walls with overspray. John and Jane Q Public both tend to take their cues from their surroundings. If the bathrooms are messy, dirty, and way too small to accommodate the crowds, then it creates a feeling of "So what?" If, on the other hand, there's care, cleanliness, and a true desire to serve the public, then I believe the public will respond—for the most part—accordingly.

Along these same lines, when theme parks recently realized that their prime demographic was shifting up, Six Flags announced that it would be spending $75 million throughout its parks to accommodate this older demographic. It intends to upgrade the bathroom facilities. Hurray! I love it. But this is a fine line to walk. While good bathrooms may encourage a return visit, I don't know anyone who chooses their entertainment options in the first place by comparing the toilet facilities. *"Oh, Honey, let's go to Weasel Stadium tonight! Their bathrooms are so much better than the ones at the Turtle Bowl.*" In other words, you have to offer entertainment and engagement first, and, as a sign of care and respect, offer good comfort facilities.

Meanwhile, back at the ballpark, what other things can be done to appeal to a Mom-fan?

Among those enhanced concessions, how about a few that sell food *not* dripping with fat? Not just as alternatives for women who are watching their weight (and do you know one who isn't?), but as alternatives for the kids, too. One Mom in my survey is looking for a vegetarian offering, such as grilled cheese or peanut butter. Heck, I'm still waiting for Dodgers Stadium just to get decent coffee. I'd be even more thrilled with a latte! It gets cold at night in the spring and a variety of hot drinks other than powdered hot chocolate and watery coffee would be welcome. How about simple things like cup holders on the seats? We Moms get tired of the people in the seats above kicking over their beer and having it run down into our bags. Maybe each seat could have a little storage shelf underneath it—not unlike those in college lecture-hall chairs—to keep the bag off the ground. And how about ticket prices? In order to pay for each lovely new Church of Baseball, will families have to buy seats for lap kids? Some ballparks insist on it now—like the Twins' Metrodome—and believe me, Moms notice. Why not take a page from the Legoland book and create Mothers Clubs? Stadiums are often beautiful islands of green in an urban sea of concrete. The minor league ballparks would really work well because they are more human-scaled and truly attractive. Create a program that makes the ballpark or football stadium a gathering place for the jogging or walking Mom and give her incentives to buy tickets and bring the rest of her family out to the park later. Finally, advertising and marketing that acknowledges the fact that Moms are buying tickets would be welcomed, too.

Never underestimate the value of an experience. Why not devise programs that, for a fee, allow family members to participate in pro sports in some way? Imagine allowing Moms to create a birthday party experience for a teenage girl around a Los Angeles Sparks practice. Sell the opportunity to be towel boy or towel girl for a night. Or allow Moms to hold birthday parties in the Tampa Bay Devil Rays dugout. Sell the opportunity to be batboy or batgirl for a night. Sell seats in the press box. Arrange for a locker room tour. Include authentic memorabilia as part of the package. Contact with your dream team in a concrete way can be a life-changing experience for a child or an adult or both—and I guarantee it is one for which Moms would pay.

Tickets! Tickets!

Learning to market to women was one of the prime objectives of the *Women and Baseball* study. After it was published, several teams got aboard the wagon. But those plans seem to have come largely to nought. For instance, one of the initiatives was to include a special section for women on the MLB Web site. I can't find it. And MLB is not alone. The NFL pioneered the NFL for Her on its Web site, but it's gone now, too. Several years ago, the NFL got cheers all around when it instituted Football 101 events at stadiums around the country. It was a way of reaching out to nonfans (many of whom were women and Moms even then) and explaining football basics to them. I couldn't find a single local instance of Football 101 still going. Learned and Johnson, in *Don't Think Pink*, argue that too often "pink campaigns" (those aimed specifically at women) include "three parts fear of turning off men and making expensive mistakes; a generous dollop of pastels, butterflies, hearts, and flowers; and a double shake of good intentions and sincerity." In their view, that's a recipe for disaster. Maybe that's what happened with the various sports initiatives. Too much pink.

Or maybe sometimes, it was just too much, period. There was a section on the NFL Web site called Football 101 in 2002, but I couldn't decide at whom it was aimed. It felt like a site for kids, very cartoonish. But in the FAQ section, where each question was multiple-choice, a busty blonde cartoon cheerleader yelled for you if you got it right. She threw her pom poms down in disgust if you guessed wrong. Surely that approach wasn't geared for Moms, or their daughters, or their (younger) sons! And forget the individual NFL team Web sites. Click on the cheerleaders tab, and what pops up is more like soft porn than useful information or family-friendly entertainment. These sites and a few female sportscasters seem to represent the NFL's entire consciousness of women, never mind Moms. (There is one notable exception, but more about the NFL Mom-as-coach experiment later.)

A quick search of the NBA Web sites is equally revealing. It must be a wonderful feeling to have such a strong fan base that no effort is needed to reach out to families or children. Neither the Lakers nor the Knicks offer any family ticketing, promotions, or even "Kids Only" sections on their Web sites. On the other hand, while the Chicago Bulls don't offer family ticket packages, at least they have a section on their Web site for kids, and even better, they have joined with the Chicago White Sox to form a sports academy for kids age four through college age. That's a brilliant way to give back to the community and develop new generations of fans. The Orlando Magic and the Utah Jazz have lots of kid-friendly promotions and special events, but I didn't uncover any family ticket packages. The Denver Nuggets get an A+ for their

$59 family-night ticket package. It includes four tickets, four pizzas, four drinks, and $10 worth of gas. Great deal! And it's the kind of deal that might encourage a family to give professional basketball a shot. As a Mom, I would be much more inclined to try pro basketball for the first time if I didn't have to spend a fortune. If the experience is a good one, I'm very likely to spend more to repeat the experience.

Then there are the teams that could offer workshops on how NOT to make a fan. Said one exasperated Mom:

I live in Los Angeles and I always theme my kids' birthday parties. When my son turned ten, I asked him what he wanted the birthday theme to be, and he said, "basketball!" I said okay, why don't I send you and your friends to a professional basketball game? I decided to get Clippers tickets. I used to be a Clippers season ticket holder, by the way. I ordered nine tickets for six kids and three adults. In the week or so before the game, I called the Clippers to ask if they could put my son's name up on the board with a happy birthday message. I said I had just bought nine tickets and that it would thrill him to see his name in lights. I knew that they did this because when I was a season ticket holder, I had them do it for my husband on his birthday. They told me they would be glad to and that it would cost me $75. Excuse me? How can it cost $75? "Well, if we didn't charge, then we'd have to do it for everybody." It didn't matter to them that I had already purchased nine tickets and that I was sending my husband with $400 in his pocket to buy food and souvenirs for the kids that day. From my point of view, they missed a golden opportunity to make a fan. Not only one little boy, who in the next 15 years will probably have disposable income for basketball tickets, but possibly five other little boys. And it certainly would have left the three adults with a good feeling. My son might even have wanted a Clippers jersey as a souvenir. Instead, he's been saving his money since then to buy a $60 Sacramento Kings jersey.

Now, the total cost of this marketing fiasco to the Clippers can't be measured unless we also consider that this Mom, who heavily influences all the decisions on family spending for sports as entertainment, will hesitate before she sends any member of her brood back to a Clippers game. She also has told at least ten of her friends how badly she was treated, and as every good marketer knows, her experience will influence those people when they face a similar decision. So the entire circle of the disaffected might reach as high as 50 or 60, or even more if her friends tell their friends. This is the L.A. Clippers, my friends! They never sell out a game. They need all the fans they can corral. Their only investment? Two minutes of time to type the greeting into the computer, along with a change in attitude from no-can-do to happy-to-help-you.

The Minors Are Major Fun

Another level of professional sports—the minors in baseball and hockey—seems to have a better grasp of family fun and entertainment, perhaps because these teams are truly community based. According to the Moms who responded to my survey, pro sports at this level are much more family friendly. There's a lot more crowd/player interaction. The organizations sponsor all kinds of events, games, between-inning contests, giveaways, and opportunities to meet players. Moms who go to both major pro sports events and minor ones enjoyed the minor ones more. The atmosphere is better. One Mom, a lifelong baseball fan, said that, at the minor league level, "they play ball for the fans." There's the fun of trying to figure out the next Wayne Gretzky or the next Mark McGwire. The setting is important, too, and many towns have built new stadiums or arenas recently that contribute to the great atmosphere. One thing is clear at the minor league level—they are glad to see fans and they treat them that way. Minor league clubs know they have to market to Mom. And don't forget, the ticket price is much more attractive for a family. A family of four can park and get tickets, food, and souvenirs for around $50 on average.

In 2002, *Time* magazine pointed out that "as family entertainment, the minor leagues are hard to beat." According to the article, minor league baseball attendance had grown 29 percent since 1992, while major league ball attendance had increased by only 3 percent.[9] Minor league team owners know that they are cultivating the next group of major league fans, but most major league organizations appear largely to have missed the point. They seem content with merchandise and TV revenues. But it is that loyal (and stagnant) fan base that watches games on TV and buys those darn T-shirts!

Rah, Rah, Sis Boom Bah!

One revelation in the results of my survey was how much Moms enjoy collegiate sports. In fact, they rate the experience of collegiate sports above that of many pro sporting events. Frances, an especially sports-savvy Mom, explained:

There's great energy at college games. They aren't overly attended and are very accessible. It's easy to walk up and get tickets for most sports; it's a little harder for the big sports like men's basketball or football. There's the added advantage of being on a college campus. It's a great way to begin to show your kids a little about college life. We are big fans, and we enjoy watching the young players grow up. It's even possible to make friends with their families and follow their careers beyond college. But maybe the best thing is the feeling of pure sports. Not that I'm saying there aren't some problems with drugs and cheating, but compared with professional sports, there's more innocence and a much better feeling about teamwork.

Andrea, who also feels that college sports are much better experiences, echoed Frances's remarks. "They offer a good role model for my children. There's a much better feeling of sportsmanship, camaraderie, and team loyalty. And you know that the money you spent on the ticket is going for a good cause—the support of the program—not some superstar's overinflated salary."

Perhaps it's naïve to think that major professional sports, which are a huge business, can fully implement the lessons of college and minor league sports. But it seems to me they ought to try. We aren't fooled by the current state of affairs, and neither are our children. All the sponsorships and big advertising deals in the world can't buy the goodwill of a single fan. That takes something extra: the ability to make the emotional connection that turns a casual observer into a rabid fan.

Connecting at the Heart

That emotional connection is at the core of the marketing relationship pro sports should have with mothers. It's a fact: Women are more interested in relationships with brands—and that's what a sports team is—than their male counterparts. The smartest retailers know this.

There is no quicker way to a mother's heart than through her child. Every time a professional team in any sport reaches down to the kids playing that sport with encouragement, tickets, speakers, gear, money, or enthusiasm, they increase their chances of making that emotional connection with Mom.

It is true that all the major sports support youth versions of their game in some way, if only by allowing their names and logos to be used. Most have special programs that reach out to underprivileged kids, and I applaud the teams and the individual players who devote their time and money to these causes. But in the interest of each game's future, why not reach out more to *all* kids, at least in each franchise's local market? Think about it: If the latest Babe Ruth showed up occasionally at Little League practices in Bedford-Stuy *and* Scarsdale, or the latest Walter Payton gave workshops to Pop Warner teams in Oak Park *and* the South Side, or the latest Kareem showed his moves to groups of L.A.-area YMCA teams in Compton *and* Woodland Hills, wouldn't that get more kids excited about their local sports opportunities? And wouldn't it persuade more Moms to buy tickets? Those jazzed kids will become adult ticket buyers, the next generation of fans. And their appreciative Moms will give the local teams a shot in the arm right away.

One of the reasons that soccer swept this country beginning in the 1980s was that it seemed a more democratic game than baseball or basketball, and it focused much more on team dynamics. Moms responded to that. Many of them (and many dads, too) had had horrible experiences with youth football, basketball, and baseball. They wanted their kids to play sports, but they didn't want them turned into competitive monsters. AYSO had a great reputation for positive coaching and controlling the controlling parent. The atmosphere just felt better. Youth soccer continues to thrive with Mom's support.

The NFL evidently noticed, and gets cheers for one attempt to interest Moms in football at that all-important grassroots level. In 1999, Scott Lancaster, senior director of Youth Football Programs for the NFL, started an experimental program in Somers, New York, to train Moms to coach children's football. According to Lancaster, "Moms are one of the greatest missing resources in coaching. Their approach is very nurturing, very inclusive, but the most important thing is that they listen."[10] This is definitely a different football from what I grew up with in Texas, where it's the state religion. The 16 Moms who made the commitment trained for 60 hours with NFL representatives. They focused on the basics of the sport plus sportsmanship and other life skills. Lancaster had realized that Moms are major obstacles to recruiting kids for football. Most of them know the injury statistics for football, so there is a lot of fear surrounding the game. The program provided a better understanding of football in general, and it emphasized things Moms like to hear: Everybody gets to play every position. It has to be fun. Good sportsmanship is important. Yell encouragement and whisper constructive criticism.

The Moms who participated loved the program. The original plan was to take it nationwide, although that doesn't seem to be happening.

Listen to Your Mother

Lancaster clearly recognized the tough hill that football has to climb, otherwise known as Mom's objections. So he reached out to Mom, the final decision maker, by stressing fun and sportsmanship for the kids and giving Mom credit for her hard-earned skills as a life coach. All the major sports need to reassess their connection to their fan base, but most of all, they need to take a cue from Lancaster and recognize Mom's role in the care and nurturing of new fans.

Endnotes

1. Eric Fisher, *Insight on the News*, July 15, 2002, vol. 18, i25, p. 28.

2. President's Council on Physical Fitness.

3. www.littleleague.org; www.soccer.org; www.popwarner.com.

4. University Interscholastic League, www.uil.utexas.edu.

5. Jennifer A. Sloan, "Marketing Sports to Women," Master's Thesis, Seton Hall University, 2001.

6. Scarborough Sports Marketing, news releases, January 22, 2001, and December 4, 2002. The figure of 50 million includes women who are very/somewhat interested in the NHL, NBA, WNBA, PGA, NASCAR, Pro Soccer, or MLB.

7. Major League Baseball news release, July 26, 2000.

8. www.phillies.com.

9. *Time*, August 12, 2002, vol. 160, i7, p. 54.

10. Gwen Morrison, "My Mom, the Football Coach," preteenagerstoday.com.

Chapter 7

Zoos, Museums, and Aquariums Spell Relief for Mom

I was born in Colorado Springs, Colorado, in the shadow of Pike's Peak. We left there when I was three, but even after we moved, we always spent our family vacations in Colorado, with my aunt and uncle. Every year until I was 18, I went back to visit such enchanted places as the Garden of the Gods, Manitou Springs, the Broadmoor Hotel, and the Cheyenne Mountain Zoo. Cheyenne Mountain was my first real city zoo experience, and I'll never forget it. I saw my first giraffe there and even fed her a rye cracker. Her tongue was soooo long and it was grey and pink. She had huge eyes with long lashes, and I fell in love. Cheyenne Mountain was also my introduction to snow leopards, which exemplify the exotic and mysterious to me. They were then, and have remained, my favorite big cats. These first zoo experiences imprinted on me like a momma goose on a gosling.

Since those days, I have been drawn to zoos all over the country, as a single adult, a married adult, a contributor, and now a Mom. I have watched zoos evolve from simple bestiaries and menageries into the Noah's Ark of the future. I've seen the cages disappear, to be replaced by enclosures and habitats. Zoos have been transformed into places that are much more human and much less inhumane. And Moms love them.

I have decided to put zoos, museums, and aquariums together because, from a Mom's point of view, they have certain things in common. First and foremost, they are almost all nonprofit organizations; the American Zoo and Aquarium Association (AZA) lists only ten for-profit institutions among its more than 200 members.[1] Without exception, they are devoted to education. And they are also all entertainment and compete for my entertainment budget, whether they will admit it or not. In this chapter, I will look at each of these venerable institutions, in turn, and point out what makes them Mom magnets. Or not. Let's start with zoos.

Zoo Stories

I'm happy to report that, in general, zoos understand Moms—maybe because they deal with so many moms of the animal variety. The AZA reports that the target audience for zoos is 25- to 49-year-old women with children. That would be Moms. Zoo management knows that the first trip to a zoo is Mom's choice. The next trip is usually at the behest of the children. Consequently, zoos are intensely aware of the power of Mom. Roger C. Birkel, the former director of the Baltimore Zoo, points out that while a zoo's first responsibility is to the well-being of the animals, the second is to the guest experience. Moms choose zoos because they know that the experience for their children—and for themselves—will most likely be a good one. It's outdoors, it's educational, it's entertaining, and it's relatively inexpensive.

The success of zoos doesn't seem to be as dependent on good customer service as that of most places that cater to families. Certainly kudos go to those zoos that have trained employees and volunteers to treat the human visitors with as much kindness and respect as the animals. They can and do make a visit more engaging and more educational. But even surly employees are unlikely to ruin completely an outing at the zoo because interaction with humans isn't a requirement of the core experience. You can *ooh!* and *aah!* over a hillside full of zebras and giraffes without speaking a word to a single employee.

Zoos encourage Mom participation early on. Many zoos have instituted walking programs for member Moms whose kids are in strollers. The Moms come early, before the zoo officially opens, and meet other Moms and children for a walk/stroll through the zoo. Mom enjoys meeting people with similar interests, and she loves the fact that the kids will be entertained in a safe environment. Once the kids are toddling, then there are more options. Across the country, zoos sponsor a variety of events that encourage small children's interest in the animal kingdom. The opportunities are engaging and very attractive—at least until the kids are about 12. A Mom couldn't ask for more.

Even for Moms who have busy work schedules, zoos are a good bet for weekends, and many zoos have started programs that open the zoo at night. Some offer family sleep-overs in the zoo. For instance, the Jungle Nights adventure at the Catoctin Wildlife Preserve and Zoo in Thurmont, Maryland, allows families and other groups to spend the night in the zoo. Others just extend hours so that the animals with nocturnal habits get a chance to show off; during the summer, the Cincinnati Zoo and Botanical Garden is open until 9:00 p.m. Some, such as the San Diego Wild Animal Park, offer music and dance programs to complement different zoo environments. The late hours and weekends make it easier for a working Mom to take advantage of all the zoo has to offer. Since education is a core value for zoos, most sponsor summer camps, special one-day programs for kids, even art enrichment classes—all with the goal of teaching the wonders of the planet by giving children a chance to get to know something about the animals with whom we share it.

It wasn't always like this. I clearly remember the first Urban Land Institute Entertainment Conference I attended in New York City in 1994. At a round table discussion hosted by Roy Shafer,[2] a zoo director was looking for ideas to use in the makeover of his large, metropolitan zoo. I offered him an experience I had had recently at Siegfried and Roy's Secret Garden and Dolphin Habitat at the Mirage Hotel in Las Vegas, where the two magicians performed. He was flabbergasted. The fact that I dared to speak the word zoo in connection with their menagerie really upset him. It seemed that the performers' efforts on behalf of the white tiger did not constitute true science, and therefore, the Secret Garden was not a good example of a true zoo. When I finally got a chance to speak, I told him that the Garden offered what most zoos at that time did not—a good story. Using a personal headset, it was possible to hear how each animal got there, the animal's name, its place of origin and some touching or funny anecdote about the animal. The story I remember most vividly from my visit was the elephant whose best friend was a chicken. Even then, it sounded like the perfect setup for a great children's book. And right in front of me were the elephant and the chicken!

My point to the outraged zookeeper was that Siegfried and Roy had made an unforgettable emotional connection between the animals and me. And zoos might benefit from a similar tactic. If zoos could personalize each visit, I felt that fundraising would be much easier. The intervening decade has told the tale. That zoo director, no doubt, has come face-to-face with reality and can now recite the names and backstories of his own zoo stars.

Before zoos could focus on telling individual animal tales, there was a lot of history to overcome. According to Birkel, when he started as a zookeeper in the 1970s, there were only a handful of zoos with education departments. Zoos were still focused on their collections and little else. In subsequent years, many zoos overcame their own defensiveness over the old ways of managing animals and moved to a holistic approach that not only included education, but obsessed over it. In too many cases, that obsession became a barrier to guests' enjoyment of their visits. "In the past, zoos pushed science to the detriment of the guest experience. They talked about species instead of individual animals," says Birkel. "Zoos have been accused of advancing at a dinosaurian pace."[3] A coldness or scientific aloofness was at work in many zoos for years, which was an improvement over the cage collection days, but still formidable. However, I believe the pace of change is picking up, and in the right direction. Many zoos have moved away from hard, dry science and embraced the idea of an emotional connection mixed with engaging science.

For instance, the San Diego Zoo had a billboard campaign in 2003 that invited guests to come and see specific orangutans. Each ape got his or her own poster and a very human descriptor. For example, one read "Unkie, the soprano!" The kids' page at the San Diego Zoo Web site also introduces the animals at the zoo by name: Victor, the echidna; Makini, the okapi; and Blanca, the white tiger, to list a few. Today, you are much more likely to find out that Charlotte, Ethel, Danny, and Shadow are Magellanic penguins that live at the Bronx Zoo, and that each has a personality. Charlotte and Ethel are shy. Danny is very social, and Shadow likes to be hand-fed with his head just out of the water. Only a few years ago the zoo community would have frowned upon such approaches.

Signage at the zoos has changed, too. In the past, the sign indicated the basic facts about the animal: where it lived; what it ate; which class, order, family, genus, and species it belonged to; and when it was acquired. Today, you are much more likely to be introduced to the animal as an individual with an intriguing story, to learn its name, and to see pictures of it with its family or group. You might discover its age and personality attributes; what foods it likes and what foods it doesn't; how it gets its medicine when it's sick; what kind of parent it is—any number of facts that bring the animal into sharp focus for both children *and* adults. You might learn that the lowland gorilla sitting in the corner has had six babies at the zoo and that her oldest son, the large male lazily stripping leaves from a branch, is now leading the group.

Not everyone is on board with the idea of an emotional connection. Some zoos refuse to name their animals, but I'd be willing to bet the zookeepers don't call the critters by their scientific names! These kinds of connections, once looked down upon as anthropomorphic abominations, merely recognize the way people really are. And as much as zoos are for animals, zoos are also for people. People like to see themselves as linked in some way to the animals. Zoos that have learned to play off this natural inclination in human groups have found greater support for their animal groups. Intellectually, I know that I should care about the welfare of the animals because we all are in this together, but when I make an emotional connection, then I know in my heart that I need to *do* something, so I buy a season pass—or send money to the World Wildlife Fund.

Zoos represent a wonderful family experience with all the things a Mom loves: a safe environment, engaging exhibitry, a deep learning experience, connections, cleanliness, lots of places to sit down to rest or to observe, and food (sometimes great, sometimes just passable). What more could a Mom want?

You recognize a loaded question when you see one, don't you?

The Teenage Animal

When it comes to good, family-friendly, Mom-targeted engagement, zoos aren't missing much. But like almost everyone else in the cosmos, they have yet to figure out teenagers. Many zoo directors consider teens a lost cause, though they come to this conclusion with great sadness and reluctance. Many teens don't seem to find zoos a congenial place, certainly not a choice to go with friends to hang out. It's hard to hold this against the zoos because, heaven knows, they have tried. Many have developed science academies for committed teens. Others have junior zookeeper programs that encourage teens to get behind the scenes at the zoo and discover what the animals and the keepers are really like. Many have opened their doors to Girl Scout and Boy Scout groups for campouts and special programs, but in the end, zoos continue to struggle to attract teens.

Teens are a tough and often fickle market. Just ask retailers. However, they are worth pursuing. It is during this period of their lives that they begin to broaden their moral sense. They start to realize that there is more to the world than what they are wearing and how their hair looks. For instance, today's teens see much more underneath the brand than you might imagine. When Nike bought Hurley, the surfboard apparel manufacturer, word spread among hardcore boarders that Nike was trying to buy into their world without properly paying its dues. Hurley's cool factor declined. Hurley was no longer authentic. So this stage in a teen's life may not be a great time to sell them on an "outing to the zoo." But it is the perfect time to sell them on the stories of the zoo: the impact of poaching, using the story of the orphan rhinoceros; or how snow leopards are endangered because human beings like to wear their fur; or the importance of zoos in maintaining the diversity of the gene pool for some species. After all, anything that deals with sex ought to attract teens!

I once had a pastor, a father of four, who was the first person to point out the obvious to me: Children love passion. They thrive on it. That passion can manifest itself as a fit of giggles or as a temper tantrum. Sometimes it's starting something and sitting back to watch it play out—like a fight between parents. Face it: teens in particular are sloshing buckets of mixed-up and sometimes inappropriate emotions, likely to cry over the outcome of their soccer tournament or crack jokes when their granddad dies. If and when zoo programs can enlist that passion and inform that teen of how best to direct it to some greater good, then we all will have won. Programs like the San Diego Zoo's InternQuest, which is designed for 11th and 12th graders interested in zoo science, are wonderful. Similar programs exist at many zoos. For example, Baltimore has Wild Explorers for ages 12 to 15, and the Wildlife Conservation Society at the Bronx Zoo has the Wildlife Science Careers Program for Girl Scouts ages 11 to 14. As a Mom, I would like to see something more for those middle-school and high-school students who are *not* the cream of the crop and who are not already members of organized youth groups—the ones who are casting about for some inspiration. Something that might persuade them to rise, as the cream does, but that is still obviously fun, not purely educational. Maybe it's out there already. Maybe I missed it.

Zoos need to give teens, like the rest of us, opportunities for intimate interaction with the animals. If you'll forgive another Vegas reference, my son vividly recalls the lions at the MGM Grand because he walked underneath them through a clear tunnel, and could see their feet and claws *this* close. Anything that brings a teen into actual contact with the animals can be a life-changing experience for him or her. Birkel noted that new zoo displays too often lack intimacy. "Guests crave interaction. They need that connection between themselves and the animals," he said. Zoos that can find that magical mix of habitat and contact, the big picture and the extreme close-up, will be the winners with Moms, teens, and everyone else.

There are some innovative ways to reach out to the teen market and still live within the budgets that restrict most zoos. One idea is partnerships involving well-established teen interests. Teens love fashion, music, video games, extreme sports, movies, and hundreds of other things. Look for partnerships that cross over. There are rock bands with social consciences. Look at U2 and Bono. The man was up for a Nobel Prize! Find a hometown equivalent. There are large audiences for the PC games that allow you build your own zoo. Look for some crossover there. Stage a fashion show featuring animal prints and faux fur for teens. For those zoo directors and their boards who want to set themselves apart and actually crack the teen market, look to the teens themselves for the answer.

Animal Theme Parks?

I know what the answer isn't—at least for me. It isn't a zoo-themed amusement park. Along with other zoophiles, I hope that zoos will resist the urge to build the world's highest, fastest roller coaster in an attempt to interest teens. It won't work. The teens might come for the roller coaster, but they aren't likely to stay for the zoo. The zoo will just be a backdrop for the thrill rides. As a Mom, I cringe at the thought of mixing the Serengeti and Six Flags. I just don't think there's any amount of marketing that could bring me in or get me to pay for my kids to go in.

I can hear you grinding your teeth. You are practically shouting at me that I just listed several crossover opportunities for zoos. Why be hypocritical and advise against a roller coaster? Because going to such an extreme, it seems to me, runs too far afield from the educational mission of zoos. The outraged zoo director I met at ULI might not believe this, but I do realize the difference between educators and entertainers. The best educators use entertainment value in the subject matter or the presentation to engage the mind and heart in learning. Entertainers often use educational value to enhance—often for Mom's sake—what is fundamentally an entertainment experience. Zoos are educational institutions whose library holdings are animals rather than books. They must devote their inevitably scarce capital resources to developing and maintaining those holdings and spend their operating funds to tell the animals' stories effectively, thereby educating the public, their students. A fashion show or concert to pull teens in and raise their consciousness of ecological issues would serve zoos' essential purposes. Using capital funds to build a roller coaster would not, because riding that coaster would divert teens' attention away from the animals, rather than directing it toward them. There are ways for a zoo to stick to its mission, and at the same time engage its audience without turning into a theme park. We have plenty of theme parks already.

So what do I do with the 600-pound gorilla that is sitting in this room marked zoos? From my point of view, Disney's Animal Kingdom is just like that horse of a different color from *The Wizard of Oz*. It is not a nonprofit, educational institution. It is part of a huge entertainment conglomerate that can add a zoo-type experience to its theme park complex without having anyone get confused over its motivation. Disney's head designer on the project, Joe Rohde, has said that Animal Kingdom is a theme park about animals, not a zoo. It's an intriguing mix of Disney characters, animatronic dinosaurs, and about 1,000 real animals. It cost almost $800 million to build. Just to put that in perspective, the total operating revenues for all zoos, aquariums, wildlife parks, and other miscellaneous animal attractions (212 institutions in all in the United States, Bermuda, and Canada) for 2000 was under $1.6 billion.[4] So yes, Disney has a wonderful animal-themed park, but comparing it to the local zoo is like comparing a new stretch Hummer limo to MacCready's Solar Challenger. They both might be great transportation, but they just ain't the same!

Also in Florida is Busch Gardens, a not-quite-as-famous animal-themed park. It has many of the same attributes: a collection of rides—most of them terrifying roller coasters—plus a variety of animal encounters that encourage close-ups with birds of all varieties, gorillas, hyenas, hippos, and other creatures. It, too, doesn't really belong in the same category as the nonprofit zoo, even though it does have some wonderful exhibits, education programs, and thousands of animals. The models that Busch and Disney provide demonstrate that entertainment companies can create animal attractions without doing violence to their own fundamental mission. But zoos are unlikely to be successful if they try to return the favor by becoming theme parks.

Museums: Engagement, Not Entertainment

In 1996, in the first issue of *The EZone*, Judy Wolfram wrote her inaugural "Culture Boom" column. We had chosen the name because it seemed that every week someone, somewhere announced plans for a new museum, zoo, or aquarium. We felt that this apparently unprecedented building spree signaled a sea change, and we intended to cover it. City governments and real estate developers were starting to look at museums in new ways as communities grappled with the age-old question of *"Who are we?"* At that time, the American Association of Museums (AAM) listed 8,000 museums in the United States. Today, it lists 16,000.[5] That's 8,000 new museums in less than ten years in the United States alone!

Museums have been around since at least the third century B.C., when everyone lined up to view the sights at the Museum of Alexandria, founded by Ptolemy I. Our past is compelling. By acknowledging where we came from, we understand better where we are and we get a glimpse of the future.

Museums today range from the incredible Smithsonian Institution, the largest museum in the world, with over 142 million objects, 16 museums, and the National Zoo in Washington, D.C., to the Spam Museum, a 16,500-square-foot exhibit on canned meat in Austin, Minnesota. In 2003, 24 million people visited one of the Smithsonian's museums or the zoo. Thirty thousand people attended the official opening of the Spam Museum.[6] There's the rub in trying to examine museums. They span the sublime to the ridiculous. Some are wonderful. Some are inspirational. Some are painful. Some are sad. They come in so many flavors that we have to categorize them before we can talk about them.

We have art museums, natural history museums, science and technology museums, commemorative museums, children's museums, corporate museums, and simply bizarre museums. What else would you call the Museum of Bad Art (MOBA) in Dedham, Massachusetts, or the Julia C. Bulette Red Light Museum (as in "brothel") in Virginia City, Nevada, or even better, the Burlingame Museum of Pez Memorabilia in Burlingame, California? Americans, it seems, will memorialize just about anything—even dirt. Yes, Virginia, there is a Museum of Dirt. It's in Boston—not the Dust Bowl country of Kansas or Oklahoma.

Americans love their museums. According to the AAM, in 2002, there were 865 million museum visits in the United States. That's more than the attendance at all the professional baseball, football, and basketball events in the country combined. Tourists especially love museums, and are willing to pay to get to them: domestic and international tourists who visit museums spend nearly twice as much on their travel as those who do not. Museums rank in the top three family-vacation destinations. And since we have established that Moms are making those vacation plans, you can see how much museums appeal to Mom.[7]

The heart of a museum, any museum, is its role as a center of learning. This passion for educating the public has given the museum world a sterling reputation. AAM says that Americans view the museum as one of the most important resources for educating our children and as one of the most trustworthy sources of objective information. Eighty-eight percent of museums provided some kind of K–12 educational programming in 2002. That translates into nearly 4 million hours of educational programs! Museums can be a vital part of a community's backbone. They can inspire, inform, challenge, and chagrin whole populations. They add immeasurably to that elusive "quality of life" we all seek.

And yet, most museums have finally admitted that they must compete with theme parks and other entertainment attractions for their audience. After all, there are only so many leisure hours in a family's week. Museums, theme parks, movie theaters, concerts, the beach, the mountains—all call to us. They might have different missions individually, but each museum is looking for a time commitment from my family and me. It has caused some distress in the museum community. These non-profit educational bulwarks have spent at least the last 25 years examining their missions, their financing, their marketing, and their exhibitry in the shadow of Disneyland. This intense self-examination continues today, but attitude changes are apparent across the nation.

As a professional in the now moribund themed entertainment business, I have had a ringside seat watching museums approach the designers and builders of theme parks for help in exhibitry. There was a time when Disney was exactly what a museum *didn't* want to be. The museum establishment cringed at the very thought! Then in the mid-1990s, Kathy Dwyer Southern, then director of what would become Port Discovery children's museum in Baltimore, hired Disney's Imagineering as museum designers. The ripples from that event still haven't stopped. The fact is, Port Discovery opened in 1998 and is very successful. It seems the Imagineers didn't do too badly.

Somewhere along the line, the old image of a museum preserving and protecting our culture and heritage in dimly lit, poorly ventilated rooms full of glass cases and typewritten labels began to give way to the modern, 21st-century idea of environmental and experiential learning. But that disconnect between user and purchaser that Pat McBride described (see the Preface) exists within the museum world, too. Some institutions understand the user and the purchaser better than others.

Children's Museums

Today's children's museums are excellent examples of the Mom Factor at work. According to Roy Shafer, "Most children's museums are the direct result of two things: The Junior League and an old house." These are museums created by mothers for mothers and their children, and even now, they are run primarily by women. They provide early learning opportunities for young children in a safe and friendly atmosphere. The age range overall tops out at about 12, and often the cap is even younger. The Please Touch Museum in Philadelphia, which has become one of the nation's top children's museums under the dynamic leadership of Nancy Kolb, is designed specifically for children seven and under. Shafer contends, and I agree, that one reason these museums are so successful with Moms is that there are Moms in charge and on staff. The Association of Children's Museums reports that it has 200 member museums and estimates that there are another 50 to 150 nonmember children's museums in the United States. The growth in the last quarter-century has been phenomenal. In 1978, there were only 38 children's museums in the United States. Between 1976 and 1990, 80 museums opened. Since 1990, an additional 100 have opened, and there are 80 new children's museums in the planning stages.

Most important, from the standpoint of developers and city governments, as of 2003, children's museums anchor 69 downtown revitalization projects in the United States. This simple fact shows better than any other statistic the power of the Mom Factor. Children are the users, clearly. But Moms are the purchasers—not necessarily ticket buyers, because many children's museums are free—but Moms make the decision on how to spend time, and money follows time. The advantage to developers and city government is clear. Children's museums represent a strong daytime audience for a redeveloped downtown. (Of course, it's not just children's museums that can fill the role of daytime attraction in redevelopment. Other kinds of museums or aquariums can also help reinvigorate the city center by attracting families.) Everybody wins! More traffic, more appeal to top-flight tenants, a good balance to the nighttime traffic, and the opportunity to create a place where community can happen.

Shafer points out that children's museums are unexpectedly beginning to fill another niche—the place where parents can meet to exchange information. It is only too obvious what adults in a children's museum have in common. And it's an easy next step to reach out to those who share your enthusiasm for children and for learning. Shafer, who is often consulted by new museums and those planning expansions, reports that some of his clients are contemplating adding a Starbucks to their plans, to facilitate adult interaction. It's clear that the distinction between the user and the purchaser is shrinking, at least in the world of children's museums.

Science and Technology Museums

Science and technology museums are another bright spot on Mom's map of entertaining and engaging excursions. The Association of Science and Technology Centers has over 400 members worldwide, more than 300 of them in the United States. Every state in the union has at least one sci-tech museum.[8] In my opinion, these museums were the first to understand the connection between education and entertainment.

That word *entertainment* has certainly powered the sales of thesauruses in this business for at least the last decade. Architects and designers were digging through them to find a word other than "entertaining" to describe "entertainment." Museum officials wanted a synonym for "entertainment" that didn't imply "entertainment." Most of all, museums didn't want their dedication to learning to be diluted or misunderstood if they were suddenly entertaining, too. So "that word" was avoided in conferences, charrettes, articles, and even phone calls.

But in the midst of these linguistic contortions, sci-tech museums were busy adding very entertaining learning experiences: simulation theaters, IMAX large-format theaters, and interactive exhibitry executed by theme-park folks or—worse—movie special-effects houses. *(Horrors!)* They embraced the idea that science could be fun and that fun could be educational. A major source of the attitude change was the Exploratorium in San Francisco. Frank Oppenheimer, the younger brother of J. Robert, founded the museum in 1969. Both brothers worked on the Manhattan Project in their younger days and, eventually, ran into the buzz saw of the House Un-American Activities Committee. Frank wound up teaching high school science in Montana after Sputnik was launched, and his "library of experiments" eventually became the Exploratorium. He was director of the museum until 1985.

The Exploratorium's 650 exhibits encourage hands-on learning, or as museums like to call it now, informal learning. I think my Mom and maybe John Dewey would have called it learning-by-doing. That's the direction most science and technology centers have taken. Those interactive exhibits can be wonderful when they are done right. The added bonus from "doing it right" is that Moms and dads love to get involved in learning science, too.

Our whole family enjoys the California Science Center in Los Angeles. My husband heads for the World of Life. My son makes for the Sky Cycle. I want to be sure I get to the Communication gallery. We all enjoyed the special exhibits on Speed and, more recently, the *Titanic* disaster. It was fascinating to watch my son and his friend Francesca go through *Titanic: The Artifact Exhibit*. First, we watched the IMAX film, *Titanica*, and then booked our passage on the ill-fated ship. The fact that the kids were issued tickets with passenger names and information made the whole thing much more compelling for them. They were very aware of the difference between first class and third class. They read the descriptions of the voyage with added interest, looking for clues about what happened to the people whose identities they had assumed for a short while. That little piece of paper provided an emotional connection to the sinking of the *Titanic* and transformed a trip to the museum into an engaging experience for two teenagers. They were caught up in the passion of the tragedy. And they weren't alone. I found myself in tears reading the letters that revealed the hopes and dreams that died that day, and so did my husband.

Just like zoos, science museums offer wonderfully diverse activities for the pre-kindergarten- to 12-year-old set. They offer summer camps, sleep-overs, field trips for schools, and outreach programs that take science to the schools. But just like zoo directors, science center directors get a little squirmy when teenagers are mentioned. I distinctly remember hearing a science museum director lamenting, "They're all ours until they reach the age of 13 or 14 and figure out how to ride the bus." The implication, of course, is that if the decision is left up to the teens, they won't be caught dead at a museum. They are off to the mall.

I have to admit that science museums are working against some pretty tough odds with most teens. First of all, by the seventh or eighth grade, they have come to equate museums with field trips and therefore—dread, dread—schoolwork. Second, museums by their definition are for nerds. The cool level is so low that it doesn't even register. So, one goal of any institution that wants to attract teens should be to raise its cool level. It doesn't have to become the hottest ticket in town. But imagine this scenario: Mom says, "We're going to the museum on Saturday to see the exhib-it on chocolate." Instead of groaning and rolling her eyes, the teenage girl says, with a sigh, "Okay." That means the cool level of the museum is about in the middle. Not bad. It may never make it all the way up to a wholehearted "Cool!" but we'll take whatever progress we can get. Subject matter is important. So is presentation. I know quite a few teens who went to the Titanic exhibit. Most reported that it was the first time they had been to the Science Center since the grade-school field trip, *and* that it was way cool! The Grossology exhibit that has been touring for several years, and the exhibit RISK! from the Fort Worth Museum of Science and History also seem like naturals for teens, if properly marketed. I'm very heartened by these engaging exhibits and trust that more of the same quality and imagination are on the way.

To get to teens even more, I suggest going where they are. If many are skepti-cal about the very idea of a museum visit being fun, then maybe museums should show up where the fun is. I live in southern California, about 45 minutes from the ocean. It occurred to me that the next time there's a surfing or volleyball challenge at the beach, maybe the Science Center ought to be there with a booth explaining the physics of waves or the effects of sun on skin. As I suggested with zoos, perhaps partnerships could be widened to include companies that already have a high cool factor with teens. I wonder if any science museum has ever partnered with skate-boarder Tony Hawk on the art and science of grabbing air? To feed teens' love of music, maybe science centers should consider inviting a rock band to herald the opening of a new exhibit on the physics of rock and roll. That might appeal to younger teens who aren't quite old enough to go to ticketed concerts, but still love the music. My favorite concept—and maybe someone has done it and I just haven't heard about it—is teaming with tech companies so that museums can act as beta sites for new games and other tech inventions. As a reward, the museum could give their teen guests special access codes for cool stuff on its Web site. (Engagement can be virtual as well as physical.) To get the goodies, teens who participate in the testing can't just play the game and run; they have to file reports so that the companies get the kind of feedback they need to assess the products. The teens could learn how games are created—both the science and the art. Undoubtedly some would get ideas about future careers from such a connection. The teens would also feel some sense of empowerment if they thought their opinions mattered to a Microsoft or an Entertainment Arts. There's a whole curriculum that could come out of this kind of public/private back-scratching. Imagine the marketing campaign: "Where can you find the only Xbox 2010? At your local science museum. Come in for a test run." Now that ought to raise the cool factor significantly. I suppose hallowed institutional dicta might limit that kind of sponsorship relationship. I know sponsorship, in general, has been a hot potato for museums for some years. But it's time to look at things with a new eye if you really want to fulfill your commitment to the *whole* community you serve.

Attracting teens may be hard sometimes, but examples of effective approaches are multiplying. Rock concerts have begun adding attractive value to the music experience by offering video games on the side. The Guggenheim Museum did essentially the same thing with its exhibit on the art of motorcycles. It pulled in people who never had been to an art museum in their lives! Maybe only 5 percent of those first-timers ever came back again. But that is 5 percent the museum would never have reached in any other way. I say, "Bravo!"

Like teens, girls seem to mystify many science and technology centers. Their approach reflects a national perception that I keep hoping will go away—that girls and science and math don't mix. According to Advocates for Women in Science, Engineering, and Mathematics (AWSEM), although women make up 45 percent of the workforce, they comprise only 16 percent of scientists. In fields like engineering and computer science, that proportion falls as low as 4 percent and 6 percent, respectively. Studies attribute this underrepresentation to lack of encouragement, support, and role models for girls in science, especially during the critical middle-school years.[9] It's a tough nut to crack because societal expectations for women in the sciences are still low. In conjunction with the National Science Foundation, several museums are designing programs specifically targeting middle-school girls. The Miami Museum of Science is working with the Dade County Public Schools to encourage and empower middle-school girls in these areas. Chabot Space and Science Center in Oakland, California, is working with schools in its area on an environmental-science curriculum for girls. The Maine Discovery Museum has an after-school program aimed at aiding girls in science education. Most of these programs are off site and computer based.

Some of the best work is being done by the Girl Scouts of America, which has a massive number of programs that utilize museum resources across the nation to introduce girls to the sciences. These programs actually require hands-on science, visits to museums and universities, and contact with female scientists who can serve as role models. This is all good news, but let me suggest Moms as an additional resource. Several programs do target parents and caregivers as well as students. But let's face it, lots of Moms in this country were discouraged from pursuing science and math courses in high school and feel really inadequate about even talking to their daughters about the sciences. Some direct effort at educating Moms about the opportunities might help turn the tide. Grab the Moms that bring their kids to the children's museums and the science and technology museums and inform them about the possibilities. Introduce Mom to the role models, too. Show her the charts that reveal where the professional shortages will be over the next ten years. Show her the salary scales for the sciences and compare them to those for other professions. If sci-tech museums enlist Mom as a supporter long before the girls get to middle school, their efforts will produce better results. Parents are still the most influential people in the lives of their children, and that's power that should be harnessed.

Natural History Museums

Natural history museums, too, often offer great family adventures. Most have left behind the musty image that prominently featured stuffed animals and dioramas. For instance, Yale University's Peabody Museum offers Indigenous People weekends, with performances and exhibits focusing on the people Columbus might have met. It also presents The Natural History of Wizards and Witches for Halloween. The Natural History Museum of Los Angeles County has had great exhibits on dogs, Machu Picchu, baseball, and chocolate. Its outreach to kids and teens follows examples set by the science and technology museums: summer camps, sleep-overs, and special classes.

Even in natural history, teens are still a mystery. Some museums in the category don't even pretend to have programs for anyone between 12 and 21. It seems to me they could use a dose of passion. That passion could come from the scientists and curators who work at the museum; it could come from exhibits that tell a compelling story; or it could come from personal connections made through the exhibitry. Whether I'm in an art museum, a natural history museum, or the Spam Museum, sometimes I need help to realize why I should care. Why is this place, this information, this stuffed moose worth my time and effort? The best way to suck me in is to tell me a story. Connect to me. Pluck my heartstrings. Move me. Make me laugh. Then you can make me think.

Art Museums

Because museums are so diverse, I can't review every type of museum and its particular attraction for Moms and families. But I do want to mention art museums, in particular, because after ages of elitism focused on the well heeled and the well educated, they, too, are beginning to see the light. They are offering lots of programs designed to instill a love of art in children and adults. Slowly, their stuffy, hushed, exclusive reputations are giving way and not a moment too soon. Their own studies have shown them that children who come to the art museum with their parents are much more likely to return as adults. So they have come up with innovations such as backpacks full of fun at the Denver Art Museum and a similar program at the Baltimore Museum of Art. Kids visiting the museum are given interactive kits that contain everything from games and puzzles connected to the exhibits, to costumes that are reflected in portraits. The National Portrait Gallery in Washington, D.C., has a kids' storytelling program that talks about the lives of the people in some of the paintings. Most museums have educational programs that they offer in conjunction with the local school districts. While in the past such a program usually amounted to a series of lectures, today, it's more likely to consist of a real artist in the classroom explaining the styles and techniques of other artists before turning the kids loose on a project of their own. My favorite example of teen-friendly programming was a show undertaken by the Whitney Museum of American Art in New York, which, by the way, trains teens as docents and tour guides. The museum hosted a group of sound artists for a "Rave Night" and invited teens to come eat, drink, dance, and hang out, and it was enormously successful. I hate to say it, but "See? I told you so!" Some enterprising museum ought to get to work on the History of Tattoos or Body Piercing as Art and Religion or even Fashion as Rebellion: The Day We Took Our Corsets Off!

Perhaps the most interesting suggestion I've heard for improving the guest experience at an art museum came from former zoo director Roger Birkel. He said that security guards should be given customer-service training. Encourage them to interact with the guests. Give them information on the artists so they can answer basic questions. All those guards, with their cold, hard stares, intimidate Moms and kids alike! Yes, I know, the Louvre and other museums have had paintings snatched off the walls during gallery hours, but still! When I take my son with me to the local art museum, I'm forever telling him, "Don't get too close! Don't look like you're going to touch them! Stand back!" We'd both die of embarrassment if one of the guards felt compelled to say something to us. Unless, of course, one of them said, "If you really like the rabbit painting, you should see our Albrecht Dürer collection on the second floor." Then we would both smile and thank him and feel more comfortable about being there and coming back.

Museums that have realized that children's voices are not a detriment to art appreciation and have quit shushing the kids are moving in the right direction. Of course, many art museums could do better on the simpler things, such as seats for viewing. Every time I go to the Los Angeles County Museum of Art, I am surrounded by elderly people. I know that they—not just I—would love the opportunity to sit and contemplate a picture. It's usually easier to find benches in the permanent collections than in the traveling exhibits. I'm sure it has to do with the ability to move people through in a timely fashion, but isn't that a bit anti-art? Isn't it supposed to be a contemplative experience?

I am also grateful to those art museums that attempt to put the art into a context. Sometimes it's as simple as music or headlines from the era or a short biographical film on the artist. I am not an art scholar, and I need help to make sure that the art connects with me on some level. And if I need help, the younger audience does, too. Those museums that understand the importance of that connection will make it easier for me as a Mom to share my love of art with my children.

Sea Lions and Jellies and Rays, Oh My!

None other than P.T. Barnum sponsored the first public aquarium in the United States in 1856. He had displayed beluga whales in New York City in 1850 and probably realized that the real, live, fascinating denizens of the deep could make him as much money as a two-headed cow or George Washington's 161-year-old-nurse. Today, the American Zoo and Aquarium Association reports that 33 of its members are aquariums and another 13 are listed in the "zoo plus aquarium" category. More than 44 million people visited these 46 institutions in 2000, compared with 66 million who went to the 137 member zoos. Obviously, aquariums are extremely popular. It's one of the reasons that there are quite a few for-profit aquariums and an entire line of ocean life–based theme parks (see Chapter 5 for an in-depth discussion of Sea World, the prime example of such parks).

I've never felt the desire to explore other planets in the solar system, but if I had my life to live over again, I would spend it exploring the world's oceans. Maybe I feel that way because I was born a flatlander with no salt water for hundreds of miles. I don't recall ever visiting an aquarium as a child, unless you count the goldfish bowl in elementary school. My first look at the seemingly alien life forms of the sea was at the old Marineland of the Pacific. It was the original home of Orky and Corky, the orcas, and Bubbles, the pilot whale. They had a fabulous aquarium with a spiral ramp around the outside so guests could see different fish at different depths. I'll never forget it.

Aquariums offer Moms and their families the opportunity to visit another world, more mysterious and even more bizarre than that of a theme park, national park, or zoo. Don't laugh, but aquariums offer depth! Babies in strollers respond to the movement of the fishes behind the Plexiglas, and adults respond to the amazing facts, the diversity, and the sheer strangeness of some of the creatures. Even teens move from the gross (male fish that carry eggs in their mouths) to the grand (otters lazily dissecting a sea anemone while floating on their backs). And the experiences in between can be just as satisfying. Most aquariums do what zoos need to do more of. They offer intimate encounters with the creatures, often in tide pools full of a variety of snails, bivalves, fish, crabs, anemones, sea stars, and other animals that don't seem to mind the gentle touch of a human hand. Many aquariums have tanks with half-dome windows: you can stick your head into the concave side of one and feel as though you are underwater, face-to-face with a grouper; or, through the convex side of another, you can see in great detail a seahorse that gallops into view only inches away. Some aquariums have been designed with clear tunnels that take very dry humans through very wet environments. Sharks and other creatures swim literally all around you. Some offer opportunities to feed the critters. My husband once fed lettuce to a nudibranch. My son's most memorable encounter was with a pool of bat rays. He was able to touch the rays as they swam past and discovered that their skin feels like velvet. Moments like these live long in the memory and make that important personal connection that leads to caring—about the animal, the environment, the planet.

Aquariums follow the same path as the other institutions when it comes to dealing with children. Kids under 12 have lots of opportunities for camps, sleep-overs, and special activities. Teens are encouraged to volunteer or participate in a variety of academy classes. But with most aquariums—as with most museums and zoos—once you turn 12, the fun activities stop and the "educational" ones begin. All these institutions could benefit from a more creative approach to teens. For instance, it's well known that teens all over need their own space. Maybe just offering an aquarium-themed teen study break during exam week would encourage some kid to look beyond the bubbles. I can see finding local sponsors for this kind of event.

As a Mom, I like the fact that aquariums offer a mostly indoor attraction, with small portions outdoors. During those hot summer months, it's nice to take advantage of the air conditioning. I could always wish for more seats, but I will say that in front of most of the largest tanks, there is usually adequate seating. I think aquariums also have some of the best stores. I know that at the Monterey Bay Aquarium, I always make a point of going to the store for books, T-shirts, and cute socks. Believe it or not, you can even find a gourmet meal at some aquariums. Again, Monterey Bay comes to mind because of the very fine Portola Café, complete with oyster bar. (I still don't know quite how they reconcile serving fish with saving sea life, but that's another story.)

Aquariums are not just good for Moms. Apparently they are very healthy for the economy, especially as development anchors. The South Carolina Aquarium opened in Charleston in 2000, after an investment of $69 million, and by 2001 was improving the local economy to the tune of $23 million a year. It's the cornerstone of the Aquarium Wharf project, located in the heart of the city and very close to restaurants and retail. Also in the South is the Newport Kentucky Aquarium. It caught my eye because it offered "Cocktails with a Splash!" gratis to adults paying admission between 6:00 p.m. and 9:00 p.m. This wonderful aquarium is the anchor of Newport on the Levee, part of a huge four-level entertainment and shopping center. Opened in 1999, it has boosted the local economy by $20 million a year. Both these projects add the cachet of strong daytime traffic to these entertainment centers, but both also enhance the nighttime atmosphere. A developer working on a project that needs local families as well as tourists in order to prosper should find these facts enlightening.

Listen to Your Mother

So where does this long ramble through institutionalized education and entertainment leave us? It's clear I saved the best for last. Zoos, museums, and aquariums are real Mom pleasers for most of the reasons on the Mom Factor list. Not only do they, as a group, offer the kind of safety, value, fun, and comfort that Moms require, but when they are on their best behavior, they also offer incredible teaching opportunities, entertainment, and the authentic, immersive experiences that we all can enjoy. Of course, there is always room for improvement. Every institution can benefit from listening to and even employing more real Moms. I know it's rare for an organization to trust the voice of its own staff as much as it does outside consultants, but it should. To these institutions I say, take advantage of the strengths you already possess. Then arrange a passion transfusion. To start the flow, look no farther than your own backyard: scientists, curators, teachers, and Moms who work with and for you can be your best marketers, if given encouragement. Please keep trying to reach the teens. Help them remember how much they loved learning when they were in kindergarten and first grade. Don't make every interaction so burdened by learning something that it isn't fun. Never forget the power of the story. It is possible to put the toughest science into a context that a general audience can understand, if you tell a story. And if that story moves me or makes me laugh, then I will most likely remember it, and that is the first step to acting on it. Finally, 'fess up. Entertainment *is* important. Every really good schoolteacher in every grade from kindergarten through college will tell you that entertainment is a legitimate way to educate.

Every institution of any size has some sort of community outreach office, director, program, or committee. I ask you, how does that office define community? Does it identify Moms as an important part of the definition? It ought to. We have the money, the time, and the influence. That's a fact that all institutions need to memorize.

Endnotes

1. American Zoo and Aquarium Association, www.aza.org.

2. Roy Shafer is the former president of COSI Columbus and an organizational coach specializing in children's and science museums.

3. Roger C. Birkel interview with the author, August 1, 2003.

4. www.aza.org/newsroom/newsroomstatistics/.

5. The AAM includes zoos, aquariums, and botanical gardens in its definition of museum.

6. "Attendance Down at Smithsonian," www.cnn.com, January 6, 2004; "SPAM Museum Jam: A Celebration to Remember," media.hormel.com, June 19, 2002.

7. American Association of Museums, www.aam-us.org/resources/general/publicinterest.cfm.

8. When doing the math on museums, zoos, and aquariums, you have to understand that many of them belong to more than one of the major professional organizations.

9. "In Their Nature: Compelling Reasons to Engage Girls in Science," www.awsem.org.

Chapter 8

Conclusion: Listen to Your Mom!

This Mom's-eye view of family entertainment has taken us from shopping and dining out to trips to the zoo and the science center, with stops at fairs and factory tours, national parks and theme parks, stadiums and aquariums along the way. The variety of choices is endless, but Mom carries with her a set of common criteria by which she makes every entertainment spending decision: the eleven elements of the Mom Factor.

You have no doubt noticed that some of these elements apply not just to Moms, but to women in general, and even—shock and amazement—dads. After all, everyone wants good customer service and good value, right? Everyone is attracted by a strong story, and nobody likes to waste time through inefficiency. Isn't that obvious? Perhaps, but even so, it bears repeating because it has escaped the notice of too many designers, developers, and analysts for too long. Besides, as you have seen throughout this book, Mom adds her own special twist to each of these universal commercial guidelines, and often Mom's standards are higher. Retailers and restaurateurs and the rest of the purveyors of family entertainment who set the bar to meet those standards will impress all comers, not just Moms.

Moreover, I would argue that Moms value other elements more than do dads and women without children: social conscience, story, connection to the heart, and in this context even learning opportunities, comfort, efficiency, and health and safety. Mom is most often the curator of the family conscience. She is the font of family stories and the best audience in the world for her little boy or girl—she knows and appreciates a good story when she sees one. Mom's heart is both literally and figuratively a source of comfort for her child from womb to birthday and beyond, and emotional connections are more likely to drive her decisions than Dad's. Teaching is a large part of her core job description every day. Mom spends more time walking the hard mall floors than Dad and treasures the little things that make her feet suffer less or speed her on her way. And dare I say it: Mom, in her role as lioness protecting her cubs, is more likely to value cleanliness and safety at the local watering hole than that big, mangy lion lounging in the wallow.

So, yes, Moms are humans, and Moms are women. But they are also a distinct group, with special characteristics, needs, and desires that should command the close attention, if not the reverence, of entertainment businesses that want their money. The Mom Factor is the key to success. Listen to Mom!

A Mom Factor Report Card

I started out asking whether restaurants, theme parks, museums and attractions, sporting venues, and other places live up to their billing as family entertainment establishments. I also promised to look at the entertainment value of malls and retail stores that have added entertainment as a way of enhancing the shopping experience. I think that the answer is clear: in the majority of cases, entertaining the whole family is still a dream. However, as the stories in this book show, performance in each type of entertainment venue varies widely, and some *do* get it. They provide the kind of inspiring examples that reassure me that improvement is certainly possible. Let's take a brief look at what businesses in each category could do to raise their collective score on the Mom Factor scale.

Retail and the Shopping Mall. Identify who your customer really is by following the money to its source and treat that source accordingly. Improve customer service. Nobody ever complains of too much good service. If you are a To-Do list retailer, pay more attention to the value triad of quality, price, and selection. Recognize that Mom's time and energy are limited and make shopping both more efficient and more comfortable. Welcome Mom's children and help Mom shepherd them. If you want to move up on the shopping continuum, make the environment and the experience more engaging and fun for both them and her. And give something back to the community.

Restaurants. Decide where your core business lies. Build on recent industry progress by making menu choices more and more healthy for both adults and kids. Welcome Mom and her kids with a trained and valued staff that can offer genuine smiles, a personal connection, and attentive service—from the manager down to the busperson. Treat *all* customers as though you want to become a tradition in their family. Cleanliness is *still* next to godliness.

Family Entertainment Attractions and Theme Parks. Moms want to buy memorable, personal, and authentic experiences for our families whenever we can. So connect with Mom's heart and her head. Remember who's buying those tickets and tokens and driving the taxi. Don't be afraid to entertain Mom! Use your venue to tell compelling stories so that your appeal becomes cross-generational. Be clean, neat, and courteous, just as your Mom taught you to be.

Sports. Reach out to Mom—don't throw barriers in her way. Recognize that she, not you, controls the turnstile for the next generation of fans—whether they watch on TV, from the stands, or from the corporate skyboxes. Remember, Mom's a big fan, too. Mom is looking for role models for her kids and when she finds them, she'll spend money so her family can spend time in their presence. Improve value by looking hard at the pricing of tickets, food, parking, and memorabilia. Create opportunities for personal interaction with the team or the traditions of the team. Legends become life lessons when you engage us in the story of the team, the players, and the fans.

Zoos, Museums, and Aquariums. Here we find the best of the bunch, from Mom's viewpoint: value, fun, experiential learning for all ages, wonderful stories, social conscience, and emotional connections all abound in the best of these places. Just don't give up on the teens. Admit you are in the entertainment business and embrace your destiny.

And Another Thing . . . . We desperately need more quantitative research specifically on the economic behavior of Mom. We need systematic national data collection efforts on all Moms, from newly minted Mommies to great-grandmothers, matri-archs of whole clans. And we need to listen more to Moms as Moms, to get their stories of pain and gain, irritation and inspiration, for the benefit of businesses and customers alike.

Right now, those Moms in America with kids at home control or influence spending by and for more than 100 million people! Another 50 million Moms buy stuff for, and exert continuing influence on, their chicks that have flown. Not to beat a stuffed teddy bear, but don't you think we deserve the time and attention?

Sit Down, Children, and Listen

This book was never meant to cover all the manifestations of Mom's economic power or even all possible forms of family entertainment. Nor was it meant to set Mom on high as the ultimate authority in all matters of commerce. I don't expect a Goth bar (although some Goths are Moms) or a local smoke shop to care much whether Moms approve of them or not. They know their markets and no doubt serve them well. The book was never meant to praise all the good businesses or slam all the bad ones. My goal was to issue a wake-up call:

First, if you are a mother reading this book, then I want you to know you have power. The kind of power the world respects: financial power. It's time to use it. We can use it to reward good service, improve our family's diet, educate and engage our children, and shape the world we live in. It's time to say, "If you want my money, then act like it."

Second, if you are creating entertainment goods or services that you think will appeal to some member of my family, don't leave me out of the equation. "Wake up and smell the hummus!" as the Genie said in *Aladdin*. You now know that I either spend or influence the spending of nearly every dollar that flies out of the family household. As a businessperson, you know that to succeed, you have to follow the money. Well, here it is—in my purse. The real trick is to get me to open my purse *and* feel good about it. You won't get far if I feel as though I'm being robbed or patronized or both.

We Moms are emotional beings with high expectations. Our circle of influence is wide and deep. We are relationship-driven, but we also have brains. We can be supportive when it seems crazy to do any such thing. We can be loyal way beyond when we should be. It comes with the territory staked out by Moms for millennia. After all, aren't we the creatures who tell our beautiful babies they can be whatever they want to be? Don't we support our children even through the teenage years when our intelligence level drops so precipitously? And isn't it Mom who defends you to the world when you change your life direction, from discovering the cure for cancer to becoming a poet or a rock star? Of course, because she's Mom, she'll also drive you nuts telling you to get a *real* job.

These traits spill over into everything we do. We'll keep the same dry cleaners forever because we've come to know the family owners and trust them. We don't even know how much they charge to press a tablecloth. We'll keep going to the same restaurant even if the food isn't quite as good as it once was because the owner knows us and always asks about our kids. We'll take our kids to the same spot in the mountains every summer because that's what our Moms did—every summer.

But it's also true that we have a dark side. To mangle Shakespeare: "If you dis us, we will leave." We are not amused when car dealers patronize us. We don't understand why attitude and arrogance should have any place in a fast-food restaurant. We will fight tooth and nail for our children's health and happiness, so the bathrooms had better be clean and the atmosphere friendly.

You know, Moms gossip—if you define gossip as the dictionary does. *A* gossip is "a companion," and *to* gossip is "to habitually reveal personal or sensational facts." We do share sensational facts, such as, "I will never take my kids to Playland again. They raised the price on their hotdogs and sodas and the bathroom is so dirty." Or, "Oh, my god! We went to an Armadillo game at the stadium the other night, and what a nightmare! It all started when they made me buy a ticket for the baby!" Or, "You've got to take the kids to the circus this year! It was such a wonderful experience! Just don't plan on eating there." Yes, that's the kind of gossiping we do. And we gossip with other mothers, our relatives, our coworkers, and even total strangers we might meet in the express line at the grocery store.

In our dealings with the world, Moms want it known that more is going on than just the transfer of dollars. When we make entertainment choices for our families, we are striving for much more than a T-shirt and a photo opportunity. We want an experience that we can endorse enthusiastically with our hearts *and* our purses. For Mom, it's got to be personal: you have to understand who I am, what's important to me, how packed my days are, how precious my time is, what I want and what I need, and maybe even what I dream of. Don't base your 21st-century entertainment creations on 20th-century ideas about who I am or who my children are. Ask me. Talk to me. LISTEN to me. I can tell you what I want and what I need and even how to package it. You have to understand that when I buy dog food and laundry detergent, I'm very likely interested in a bargain. When I buy memories for my family, I'm interested in making sure that they are golden memories, the kind that last a lifetime. The kind that lead to family traditions and touch the heart. Memories so wonderful and precious that there are no regrets about the cost of the plane tickets, the hotel, the silly hats, the stuffed toys, or the T-shirts. Often these kinds of memories have roots that go way beyond what a purveyor of family entertainment can imagine. The great ones reach back over the generations.

When I was about six or seven, my mother and father drove the family from Texas to New Jersey so that my mother could see one of her dearest friends from her Army days. It was during that trip that I first saw New York City. I remember looking up and up and up at the tall buildings. I also remember following the pigeons around and telling them to "Sit!" My mother had worked and played in New York for five years after the war, and her stories about those times and that place became as precious to me as my favorite fairy tales. She told me about ice skating at Rockefeller Center, going to Giants games at the Polo Grounds, seeing William Shatner as a mere babe on Broadway, and the miracle of live elephants and camels at Radio City Music Hall at Christmas.

For the next ten years, whenever I planned my future, it always included the Big Apple. I was going to be an actress! A star on Broadway! Mom not only understood my dreams, she encouraged them. When I graduated from high school, she let my drama teacher (a good friend) and me go to New York for two weeks of theater and museums and worldliness. She sent us with a list of "musts," including a visit to Mamma Leone's Ristorante and advice about the subway. We stayed with the same best friend in New Jersey, and I came home with my own tall tales about the bright lights and the big city.

Over the intervening years, life happened, but Mom and I always talked about going back together. We got our chance at a conference in 1988. What made that trip memorable was that while we were there, the Dodgers (another passion we shared) defeated the Oakland A's in Game 1 of the World Series on Kirk Gibson's beautiful home run. Mets fans were mad because they weren't in the Series thanks to the Dodgers, but New York is a baseball town and the game was on in every bar around Times Square. Mom and I (and our respective husbands) barhopped the whole night so we could watch the game. We would order a drink, cheer for the Dodgers, get "the look," and go to the next bar.

Once I went into business for myself, I was in New York at least once a year for conferences. I even got a chance to take my husband to Mamma Leone's for that romantic dinner. Then I gave birth to Benjamin.

It doesn't seem possible that a love of New York City could be genetic. But somehow I passed it on to Benjamin. Maybe it had something to do with the fact that I bought him a yellow toy taxicab and a book about the wonders of the city, including a picture and explanation of FAO Schwartz. The magic my mother had created for me began to pull him, and even as a very little boy, he talked and talked about going to New York.

It was the summer of 1999, a year after Mom's death, before I finally had an opportunity to take my son to New York. He was nearly nine. It was a short but incredible trip and the Big Apple didn't disappoint. We went to the top of the Empire State Building and tried to imagine King Kong or a dirigible like the Hindenburg hanging off the top. We gawked like good tourists at the marvelous Chrysler Building, the awesome World Trade Center, and New Jersey. We ate ice cream and walked under the 59th Street Bridge. We buzzed around the island of Manhattan in the biggest speedboat I've ever seen! We rode the subway, took taxis, ate pizza by the slice, and walked through Central Park. We toasted Mom and promised to come back to see and do all the other things. A tradition was born.

Not everyone in family entertainment can hope to create such a rich set of experiences. But listening to stories like these from Moms all over, they can begin to learn how to tap into the economic power of the Mom Factor.

Now finish your milk and help clear the table.